Fr Jerry
937.272-6083

At the Supper of the Lamb

A Pastoral and Theological Commentary on the Mass

Paul Turner

LITURGY TRAINING PUBLICATIONS

Liturgical texts in this book are published by authority of the
Committee on Divine Worship,
United States Conference of Catholic Bishops.

Excerpts from the English translation of *The Roman Missal* © 2010, International Commission on English in the Liturgy Corporation (ICEL); excerpts from the English translation of *The General Instruction of the Roman Missal* © 2010, ICEL. All rights reserved.

English translation of the *Catechism of the Catholic Church* for the United States of America Copyright © 1994, United States Catholic Conference, Inc.—Libreria Editrice Vaticana. English translation of the *Catechism of the Catholic Church Modifications from the Editio Typica* Copyright © 1997, United States Catholic Conference, Inc.–Libreria Editrice Vaticana. Used with permission.

Excerpts from the *Constitution on the Sacred Liturgy* from *Vatican Council II The Basic Edition: Constitutions, Decrees, Declarations*, edited by Rev. Austin Flannery, OP, copyright 2007, Costello Publishing Company, Inc., Northport, NY, are used by permission of the publisher, all rights reserved. No part of these excerpts may be reproduced, stored in a retrieval system, or transmitted in any form or by any means electronic, mechanical, photocopying, recording, or otherwise, without express permission of Costello Publishing Company, Inc.

Scripture quotations and references are from *New Revised Standard Version Bible: Catholic Edition*, copyright © 1989, 1993 National Council of the Churches of Christ in the United States of America. Used by permission. All rights reserved.

The image on the cover is a depiction of Revelation 7:9, " . . . there was a great multitude that no one could count, from every nation, from all tribes and peoples and languages, standing around the throne and before the Lamb, robed in white, with palm branches in their hands." The image is a photograph of a stained glass window in Saint John's Basilica, Des Moines, Iowa. Photo © Father Gene Plaisted, The Crosiers.

Photo of Paul Turner © Sara Long with Joyful Photo: www.joyfulphotoco.com.

AT THE SUPPER OF THE LAMB: A PASTORAL AND THEOLOGICAL COMMENTARY ON THE MASS © 2011 Archdiocese of Chicago: Liturgy Training Publications, 3949 South Racine Avenue, Chicago IL 60609; 1-800-933-1800, fax 1-800-933-7094, e-mail orders@ltp.org. All rights reserved. See our Web site at www.LTP.org.

Printed in the United States of America.

Library of Congress Control Number: 2011921456

ISBN 978-1-56854-921-7

ASL

IN MEMORIAM

ERNESTI J. FIEDLER

GEMMVLA CONCILIO VATICANO SECVNDO PERITI

QVI STVDIO PROPRIO ET PRÆDICATIONE PVBLICA

IN CHRISTIFIDELIBVS, STVDENTIS, NECNON DIACONIS

EAM FACIEBAT FLORESCERE

ET QVI SPEM AUCTORIS IN FRVCTVS EIVS PLENITVDINEM SVSTINAVIT

I wish to thank

Bruce Harbert, who invited

Thomas Sullivan, who referenced

Visitation Church, which discussed

Gerard Moore, Keith Pecklers, and Beatrice Santner, who read

the people of St. Munchin and St. Aloysius Churches, who communed

God, who sends us forth from the Supper of the Lamb.

PT

Table of Contents

Introduction

On that day when those invited come to feast at the supper of the Lamb, on that day when worshippers thunder mighty Alleluias, when the Lamb marries his bride in white linen, and when those who hold the testimony of Jesus witness his triumph[1]—there will be joy, celebration, music, silence, dialogue, acclamation, and prayer. All will be swept up in the glory of God. No one will have to learn what to do.

But until that day, we mortals gather at the supper of the Lamb on earth, in houses of worship, with our flawed capabilities, to worship God as best we can and to give thanks for the greatest miracle of all—the marriage of Christ with the Church, the Eucharist, the banquet in which we feast with delight on the Lamb of God who unites with us. For now, we all have to learn what to do.

The celebration of the Eucharist has been handed down to us from the apostles.[2] Throughout history the faithful have observed it according to their own cultures, climes, and traditions. The Roman Rite has experienced stages of slow and rapid evolution. In 1969, the language of the liturgy returned to the vernacular of the worshippers and the shape of the liturgy reacquired a simpler form. More options were provided to inspirit the celebration of particular assemblies for certain occasions and locales. Their active participation was restored to the heart of liturgical prayer.

> The rite of the Mass is to be revised in such a way that the intrinsic nature and purpose of its several parts, as well as the connection between them, may be more clearly shown, and that devout and active participation by the faithful may be more easily achieved.
>
> To this end, the rites are to be simplified, due care being taken to preserve their substance. Duplications made with the passage of time are to be omitted, as are less useful additions. Other parts which were lost through the vicissitudes of history are to be restored according to the ancient tradition of the holy Fathers, as may seem appropriate or necessary.
>
> —*Constitution on the Sacred Liturgy* (CSL), 50

> It is very much the wish of the church that all the faithful should be led to take that full, conscious, and active part in liturgical celebrations which is demanded by the very nature of the liturgy, and to which the Christian people, "a chosen race, a royal priesthood, a holy nation, a redeemed people" (1 Pet 2:9, 4-5) have a right and to which they are bound by reason of their Baptism.
>
> In the restoration and development of the sacred liturgy the full and active participation by all the people is the paramount concern, for it is the primary, indeed the indispensable source from which the faithful are to derive the true Christian spirit. Therefore, in all their apostolic activity, pastors of souls should energetically set about achieving it through the requisite formation.
>
> —CSL, 14

The first translation of the Mass from Latin into the vernacular gave English-speakers words to express their faith and to celebrate their unity. Now, after forty years of usage, a second English translation has appeared. This event has occasioned

---

1   See Revelation 12:1–10.

2   See 1 Corinthians 11:23.

a renewed interest in the Mass, its parts, its purposes, and its history. Many parishes are evaluating their celebration of the Eucharist to infuse it with new life, to deepen their appreciation of its meaning, and to attract both experienced and inexperienced worshippers into an encounter with Christ.

This book will help you understand the parts of the Mass so that you may enter them more intentionally and prepare for them with wisdom. It is not a pure history or commentary, though there are elements of those fields. It is an invitation to worship, a call to new intention, a deeper awareness of the privilege we share to be invited to the supper of the Lamb.

The outline of this book follows the Order of Mass in *The Roman Missal*. *The Roman Missal* contains all the prayers and rubrics to be observed in the celebration of Mass in any situation. Most of the Missal is the collection of prayers that change from one Mass to the next. But nestled in the middle are the parts of the Mass that do not change—the dialogues between the priest and the people, the four main Eucharistic prayers, the acclamations, and texts that fill up the typical "script" we follow from the Sign of the Cross at the beginning to the dismissal at the end. That is called the Order of Mass.

The parts of the Order of Mass are numbered in *The Roman Missal*, and this book is structured according to those same numbers. You will also find here excerpts from the *General Instruction of the Roman Missal* (GIRM), the introductory material that explains much more than the few rubrics from the Order of Mass. You will also read something of the history of each part of the Mass, and you will see questions that invite you to think about how you and your worshipping community can participate at Mass even better than you already do.

You will see what all worshippers have in common—a love for the Eucharist, hope in God, a desire to give praise, and a longing for the day when we will gather with Christ at the greatest banquet of all.

About the Author

Paul Turner is the pastor of St. Munchin parish in Cameron, Missouri, and its mission, St. Aloysius in Maysville. A priest of the diocese of Kansas City–St. Joseph, he holds a doctorate in sacred theology from Sant' Anselmo in Rome. He is the author of many pastoral resources about sacraments and the liturgy.

Abbreviations

AAS   *Acta Apostolicae Sedis.* Vatican City.

AC   *Didascalia et Constitutiones Apostolorum.* Ed. Franciscus Xaverius Funk. Turin, Italy: Bottega d'Erasmo, 1979.

AT   Bradshaw, Paul; Johnson, Maxwell E.; and Phillips, L. Edward. *The Apostolic Tradition: A Commentary.* Ed. Harold W. Attridge. Minneapolis, Minnesota: Augsburg Fortress, 2002.

Barba   Barba, Maurizio. *La riforma conciliare dell' "Ordo Missae": Il percorso storico-redazional dei riti d'ingresso, di offertorio e di comunione.* Rome, Italy: Edizioni Liturgiche CLV, 2008.

CCC   *Catechism of the Catholic Church* for the United States of America © 1994, United States Catholic Conference, Inc.—Libreria Editrice Vaticana. English translation of the *Catechism of the Catholic Church Modifications from the Editio Typica* Copyright © 1997, United States Catholic Conference, Inc.—Libreria Editrice Vaticana.

CCL   *Corpus Christianorum—Serie Latina.* Turnhout, Belgium: Brepols, vol. 1, 1954.

CSL   *Constitution on the Sacred Liturgy (Sacrosanctum Concilium). Vatican Council II The Basic Edition: Constitutions, Decrees, Declarations.* Ed. Austin Flannery. Northport, New York: Costello Publishing Company, 2007.

DMC   *Directory for Masses with Children.* Congregation for Divine Worship. Vatican City, 1973.

DOL   *Documents on the Liturgy 1963–1979; Conciliar, Papal, and Curial Texts.* International Committee on English in the Liturgy. Collegeville, Minnesota: Liturgical Press, 1982.

Gelasian   *Liber sacramentorum romanae aeclesiae ordinis anni circuli.* Ed. Leo Cunibert Mohlberg. Rerum Ecclesiasticarum Documenta. Rome, Italy: Casa Editrice Herder, 1981.

GIRM   *The General Instruction of the Roman Missal.* Chicago, Illinois: Liturgy Training Publications, 2011.

LP   *Liber pontificalis, Le.* Ed. L. Duchesne. Paris, France: E. de Boccard, 1955.

OM   *The Order of Mass.* International Committee on English in the Liturgy, 2008.

OR   *Les Ordines Romani du haut moyen age.* Ed. Michel Andrieu. Louvain, Belgium: Spicilegium Sacrum Lovaniense, 1971.

PG   *Patrologiae cursus completus.* Ed. Jacques-Paul Migne. Series Graeca. Paris, France: J.-P. Migne, vol. 1, 1857.

PL   *Patrologiae cursus completus.* Ed. Jacques-Paul Migne. Series Latina. Paris, France: J.-P. Migne, vol. 1, 1841.

RS   *Redemptionem Sacramentum.* Congregation for Divine Worship and the Discipline of the Sacraments. Vatican City, 2004.

SChr   *Sources Chrétiennes.* Paris, France: Éditions du Cerf, vol. 1, 1941.

THE INTRODUCTORY RITES

ENTRANCE CHANT, PROCESSION, SIGN OF THE CROSS, AND VENERATION OF THE ALTAR

1.   When the people are gathered, the Priest approaches the altar with the ministers while the Entrance Chant is sung.

When he has arrived at the altar, after making a profound bow with the ministers, the Priest venerates the altar with a kiss and, if appropriate, incenses the cross and the altar. Then, with the ministers, he goes to the chair.

When the Entrance Chant is concluded, the Priest and the faithful, standing, sign themselves with the Sign of the Cross, while the Priest, facing the people, says:

In the name of the Father, and of the Son, and of the
     Holy Spirit.

The people reply:

Amen.

The rites that precede the Liturgy of the Word, namely, the Entrance, the Greeting, the Penitential Act, the *Kyrie*, the *Gloria in excelsis (Glory to God in the highest)* and Collect, have the character of a beginning, an introduction, and a preparation.

Their purpose is to ensure that the faithful, who come together as one, establish communion and dispose themselves properly to listen to the Word of God and to celebrate the Eucharist worthily. . . .

—*General Instruction of the Roman Missal* (GIRM), 46

See also GIRM, 40, 47, 48, 49, 50, 104, 120, 122, 123, 124, 172, 173, 174, 188, 195, 273, 274, 275a, 276, 277, 294, 307, and 310.

Background

The Order of Mass begins with a succinct premise: "When the people are gathered." The Latin text says it in two words: "*Populo congregato.*" This replaces the first two words of the Order of Mass from before the Second Vatican Council: "*Sacerdos paratus,*" which means, "When the priest is ready."

The contrast is obvious, and it unveils one of the main values of the revised Missal, the active participation of the people. The rubrics, so long focused on the responsibilities of the priest and other liturgical ministers, now acknowledge that everyone's participation is critical. Mass begins not just when the priest is ready, but when the people have gathered.

Even the word "gathered" implies something more than "being ready." The people come together for a purpose. Furthermore, they are coming from someplace—from the many activities of the week, both those that have put their faith into service, and those that have sadly lured them away from Christ. The Eucharist is the source and summit of their lives, so they gather to acknowledge the events of the past week and to receive sustenance for the week ahead.

The very first words of the Order of Mass allude to the Second Vatican Council's *Constitution on the Sacred Liturgy* (CSL), which sought the "full pastoral effectiveness" of "Masses celebrated with the faithful assisting."[1]

Throughout the rubrics, the presiding minister is called "the Priest," not "the celebrant." The word "celebrant" had formerly been used in the descriptions of a Mass without a congregation. The word "Priest" establishes his role in relation to the people for whom he presides.[2]

Ministers make the procession to the altar. The order of entrance is explained in the *General Instruction of the Roman Missal* (GIRM) 120 and 172. In early Christianity the Eucharist took place in homes, so no procession was necessary. Once the celebration moved into churches, a procession evolved. It took the shortest route—from the sacristy to the sanctuary. Now the procession frequently moves through the body of the assembled people.

The Entrance Chant accompanies the procession. This was certainly the reason for its appearance in the liturgy, though its purpose was later abandoned.

---

1   CSL, 49. Maurizio, Barba, *La riforma conciliare dell' "Ordo Missae": Il percorso storico-redazionale dei riti d'ingresso, di offertorio e di comunione* (Rome, Italy: Edizioni Liturgiche CLV, 2008), p. 491.

2   Barba, p. 491.

Singing has always enlivened Christian worship. The Last Supper concluded with a hymn.[3] Paul and Silas sang hymns while they were held in prison in Philippi.[4] In the early second century, the Emperor Trajan received a letter from the pagan Pliny the Younger, who described the habits of Christians, one of which was singing in alternation a hymn to Christ "as if he were God."[5]

It is not certain when the Entrance Chant or Introit entered the history of the Mass, but the *Liber pontificalis,* an unreliable history of papal activities first recorded in the sixth century, attributes the decision to Pope Celestine I (+432). "He decreed that the 150 Psalms of David be sung antiphonally by all before the sacrifice; this had not been done before."[6] Honorius of Autun (+ 1151) says that Pope Gregory the Great (+604) added the antiphon to Celestine's Introit.[7] *Ordo Romanus I*, compiled by the eighth century, but possibly describing the Mass of Gregory the Great, calls for an Introit that encompasses an antiphon that may have preceded and concluded a Psalm, with a "Glory be to the Father" at the very end. All this accompanied the papal procession.[8] In time the procession became shorter, the antiphon became more ornate, and the verses were reduced.

Gradually, certain antiphons were assigned for specific days. Each Sunday became known by the first word of its Introit, just as some books of the Old Testament got their titles from the opening word of the first verse, and many Church documents from encyclicals to instructions are known by the opening phrase in Latin. Some celebrations of the Mass are still called by the first word of the Introit: *Gaudete* on the Third Sunday of Advent and *Laetare* on the Fourth Sunday of Lent. A funeral Mass is a "Requiem" because of its Introit.

Prior to the Second Vatican Council, the priest recited the Introit after the prayers at the foot of the altar and just before the Kyrie. In its reforms the Council restored the Introit to its original purpose—"to open the celebration, foster the unity of those who have been gathered, introduce their thoughts to the mystery of the liturgical time or festivity, and accompany the procession of the Priest and ministers."[9]

Although a text is supplied for each Mass, another song may substitute for it.[10] One option is for the priest to adapt the Entrance Chant into his introductory remarks for the Mass following the greeting and before the Penitential Act. This seems inspired by the pre-conciliar practice in which the priest recited the text himself just before the Kyrie.

During the procession, the *Book of the Gospels* may be placed on the altar. Honor has been shown to this book at least since the fifth century. In describing the Council of Ephesus (431), Saint Cyril of Alexandria (+444) says that "the holy Synod, assembled at the holy church dedicated to Mary, set up Christ in some way as a member and the head. In fact, the venerable Gospel was placed on a holy throne."[11] Setting

Singing has always enlivened Christian worship.

the book on the altar today unites two primary symbols of Christ, each one brought to a climax during the Liturgy of the Word and the Liturgy of the Eucharist respectively.

A series of gestures shows respect for the altar. The ministers bow to it, the priest kisses it, and he may also incense it. This veneration takes place before the priest goes to his chair.

The Church recognizes that kissing the altar may be offensive in some cultures. The GIRM permits conferences of Bishops to propose a different sign of reverence for approval from the Apostolic See.[12]

From at least the time of Ambrose (+397), the altar has been esteemed as a symbol for Christ. "For what is the altar of Christ if not the image of the Body of Christ?" "The altar represents the Body [of Christ] and the Body of Christ is on the altar."[13]

3 See Matthew 26:30 and Mark 14:26.

4 See Acts 16:25.

5 *Letter* 10:96. See, for example, Robert Cabié, *History of the Mass* (Portland, Oregon: Pastoral Press, 1992), p. 10.

6 LP I:230; translation Paul Turner (PT).

7 *Gemma animae* I:87, (PL 172:572); translation PT.

8 OR I:44, 50, 51.

9 GIRM, 48.

10 Ibid.

11 *Apologeticus ad Theodosium Imp.*, PG 76:471–472; translation, PT.

12 GIRM, 273.

13 Ambrose, De sacramentis 4:2, 7 and 5:2, 7. Cited in *Catechism of the Catholic Church* (CCC), 1383.

Still, there is no evidence for venerating the altar in the earliest days of the Church. *Ordo Romanus I* called for the Bishop to kiss the *Book of the Gospels* and the altar.[14] In the eleventh century a prayer was added acknowledging the relics of the saints retained in the altar.[15]

The Bible records many instances when people used incense to enhance their prayer. Aaron presented a bull as a sin offering for himself, placing two handfuls of sweet incense on the fire before the Lord.[16] Zechariah offered

These opening rites are a simplification and restructuring of the prayers at the foot of the altar that started the Mass in the Missals from 1474 to 1962.

incense at the altar of the Lord.[17] In John's vision, an angel with a golden censer offered a great quantity of incense with the prayers of all the saints on the golden altar before the throne of God.[18]

By the sixth century, Pseudo-Dionysius noted that incense was used at worship, its sweet aroma filling the room.[19] *Ordo Romanus I* says the subdeacon carried incense in procession ahead of the Bishop.[20] Candles were placed on the altar by the twelfth century, and a cross by the thirteenth century.[21] The incensation of the altar was added in the same period.[22] The rules for incensing became more elaborate in the 1570 Missal (the one following the Council of Trent), but they have been lightened in the current one. When preparing the new rite in 1965, advisors considered having the priest incense not just the altar, but also the people, upon entering the sanctuary.[23] However, the traditional practice was retained.

The priest goes to his chair after venerating the altar. This changed the practice from the 1962 Missal, where he conducted the whole first part of the Mass at the right side (the liturgical south side) of the altar. In today's practice, he takes his chair, where he assumes his role as presider over the people who have assembled for worship, and where he is prepared to pray together with them.

The Sign of the Cross had entered devotional practice among Christians as early as Tertullian (+220). "At every step and forward motion, at every arrival and departure, when dressing, putting on shoes, bathing, eating, lighting lamps, going to bed, when sitting still—whatever common thing occupies us, we mark our forehead with the sign [of the cross]."[24] The traditional words that accompany the gesture are inspired by Jesus' farewell and command to the disciples on the occasion of his Ascension.[25]

The Sign of the Cross at the beginning of Mass dates to the fourteenth century.[26] In the 1570 Missal it was entirely assigned to the priest, who made the gesture while reciting the words himself.

Pope Paul VI appointed the Consilium, a special committee to oversee the revised liturgy after the Second Vatican Council. The Order of Mass was entrusted to a group of experts known as Study Group 10.

The members of Study Group 10 considered several options for the Sign of the Cross. In 1965, the group proposed having the priest make the gesture—without saying any words—upon arriving in the sanctuary and before venerating the altar.[27] In this way, the first words spoken by the priest and the people would be the greeting. This seemed too spare, so in 1968 it was proposed that the priest and the people say the words out loud.[28] A few months later, at the request of Pope Paul VI, the words were turned into a dialogue, the priest saying almost all the words, and the people answering, "Amen."[29] Some were concerned that naming the Trinity out loud would cause a duplication with the words of the greeting that followed.[30]

---

14 OR I:51.

15 The *Oramus te, Domine*, Cabié, *History*, p. 89.

16 See Leviticus 16:11–13.

17 See Luke 1:9.

18 See Revelation 8:3.

19 *De hierarchica Ecclesiastica* 3:3 (PG 3:428).

20 OR I:46.

21 Theodor Klauser, *A Short History of the Western liturgy: An Account and Some Reflections*, (Oxford: Oxford University Press, 1965), p. 101.

22 Guy Oury, *La Messe de S. Pie V á Paul VI*, (Solesmes: 1975), p. 82.

23 Barba, pp. 249 and 375.

24 *De corona*, 3,4, CCL 2:1043; translation PT.

25 See Matthew 28:19.

26 *Cistercian Missal*, Schneider (*Cist. Chr.*, 1926), p. 253. Cited in Jungmann 1:296.

27 Barba, p. 243.

28 Ibid., p. 244.

29 Ibid.

30 Ibid., p. 245.

An alternative was proposed, having the priest say, "In the name of the Father and of the Son and of the Holy Spirit—grace and peace be with you," to which the people would respond, "And with your spirit."[31] It was even proposed that the Sign of the Cross would be said silently on those occasions when the Introit was sung.[32] The dialogue that prevailed was a novelty; the Sign of the Cross had not existed this way in any other liturgical tradition. French and German-speaking countries ultimately chose a modified solution: They assigned the complete text to the priest, including the Amen, while all made the gesture together. But English speakers joined the great majority of other vernacular languages and kept it in dialogue form as it has appeared in Latin ever since 1969.

These opening rites are a simplification and restructuring of the prayers at the foot of the altar that started the Mass in the Missals from 1474 to 1962. The priest recited various private prayers throughout the Middle Ages, and these became fixed in the 1570 Missal. But the 1970 Missal introduced here the participation of the people, the elimination of parts judged unnecessary, and the reordering of elements to improve the content and purpose of the beginning of the Mass.

31 Barba, p. 672.
32 Ibid., p. 238.

Questions for Discussion and Reflection

1. How do the people gather in your church? Do they arrive on time? How do they form a community before they take their places? How have they participated in the mission of the Church in the past week?

_____

_____

_____

2. How do the priest and ministers approach the altar? How does the Entrance Procession set the tone for Mass?

_____

_____

_____

3. Who chooses the music for the Entrance Chant and how is the decision made? How well does the song achieve its goals?

_____

_____

_____

4. According to GIRM 49 and 274, is it appropriate for ministers to bow or genuflect when they reach the sanctuary of your church? Is there uniformity among the various ministers from one Mass to the next?

_____

_____

_____

5. On what occasions do you use incense? How do you decide on the community's annual incense schedule?

_____

_____

_____

6. How have you decided where to place the presider's chair in your sanctuary?

_____

_____

_____

7. Do all make the Sign of the Cross with the priest? Is it done intentionally? Does the priest say "Amen"—or do the people? How strong is the response?

_____

_____

_____

GREETING

2.   Then the Priest, extending his hands, greets the people, saying:

The grace of our Lord Jesus Christ,
and the love of God,
and the communion of the Holy Spirit
be with you all.

Or:

Grace to you and peace from God our Father
and the Lord Jesus Christ.

Or:

The Lord be with you.

The people reply:

And with your spirit.

In this first greeting a Bishop, instead of The Lord be with you, says:

Peace be with you.

When the Entrance Chant is concluded, the Priest stands at the chair and, together with the whole gathering, signs himself with the Sign of the Cross. Then by means of the Greeting he signifies the presence of the Lord to the assembled community. By this greeting and the people's response, the mystery of the Church gathered together is made manifest. . . .

—GIRM, 50

See also GIRM, 50, 40, and 124.

Background

The priest chooses one of three options to greet the people, and they make a common response. The greetings are all inspired by scripture. The first comes from 2 Corinthians 13:14. The second can be found in several of Paul's letters, including Romans 1:7, 1 Corinthians 1:3, 2 Corinthians 1:2, Galatians 1:3, Ephesians 1:2, Philippians 1:2, 2 Thessalonians 1:2, and Philemon 3.

The final option, "The Lord be with you," is found in several places in the Old Testament, such as Judges 6:12, where it offers consolation to Gideon, and Ruth 2:4, where it seems to be a common greeting to workers. It also appears in the New Testament, for example when the angel Gabriel greets Mary in Luke 1:28. Jesus is announced as Emmanuel, "God is with us" (Matthew 1:23). At his Ascension, Jesus promised to be with his followers.[1]

When a Bishop greets the people, he says, "Peace be with you," a greeting used by the risen Christ.[2] Pope Innocent III (+1180) assigned this greeting to Bishops as the vicars of Christ, using the first words he spoke to the disciples after the Resurrection. Priests, he continued, say "The Lord be with you." People respond with words drawn from the New Testament, "And with your spirit."[3]

This reply, "And with your spirit," is more mysterious. It is based on the conclusion to these letters of Saint Paul: 2 Timothy 4:22, Galatians 6:18, Philippians 4:23, and Philemon 25. Paul prays that the Lord will be with the spirit of those who receive his letters. He says goodbye with a spiritual appeal, not a sentimental one. Only in the case of 2 Timothy does Paul use the singular form; in all other instances, he hopes that the Lord will be with the spirit of the entire community, imitating the advice he gives the Philippians, "Let the same mind be in you that was in Christ Jesus,"[4] and to the Colossians, "whatever you do, in word or deed, do everything in the name of the Lord Jesus."[5]

The liturgical greeting and response split the words of Saint Paul. The greeting is justifiably dislodged because of its Old Testament counterpart. The response of the people probably means to echo the same theme that the greeting sounded. Judging from the biblical context, the priest probably says nothing less to the people than they say to him; both imply, "The Lord be with your spirit." But the phrase is divided for the sake of symmetry and variety. The usage of the word "spirit" connects the greeting to its biblical roots, its historical usage, and the spiritual nature of the events about to take place.

The dialogue appears in the Eucharistic Prayer from the *Apostolic Tradition*,[6] probably by the fourth century, and it was eventually adopted for the greeting at the beginning of the celebration. In a homily for Holy Saturday probably dating to the same period, Christ—between his death and Resurrection—goes in search among the dead for Adam. When they see each other, Adam calls out to the others, "My Lord [be] with [you] all." Christ responds to Adam, "And with your spirit."[7]

Saint Augustine describes his entrance to the church one Easter Sunday morning when the miraculous healing of a member created a frenzy. Augustine says he "greeted the people,"

The usage of the word "spirit" connects the greeting to its biblical roots, its historical usage, and the spiritual nature of the events to take place.

though it is not clear if this was a liturgical greeting or a human one, and when silence was restored the readings from scripture began.[8]

Saint John Chrysostom says when he entered the church he said, "Peace to you," and people answered, "And with your spirit."[9] Narsai (fifth century) says the response gives the name "spirit" not to the soul of the priest but to the Spirit he has received through the laying on of hands.[10] As usage evolved, it was restricted to dialogues begun by an ordained deacon or priest, though even today the Order of Mass does not capitalize the word "spirit" in this response. The idea that it refers to the Holy Spirit of the ordained surely would have surprised Saint Paul, who prayed that the Lord Jesus would be with the "spirit" of all the faithful.

This dialogue appeared in the 1474 Missal as part of the prayers at the foot of the altar, and again after the priest kissed the altar. The 1570 Missal retained this double usage.

Study Group 10 considered moving the greeting between the Kyrie and the Gloria to

---

1   See Matthew 28:20.

2   John 20:19, 21 and 26.

3   *De sacro altaris mysterio* 2:24 PL 217:812.

4   Philippians 2:5.

5   Colossians 3:17.

6   This was an early Church order offering rules on morality, liturgy, and Church structure.

7   *Homilia II in sabbato magno* PG 43:461–462. See the Office of Readings for Holy Saturday.

8   *City of God* 22:8, CCL 48:826.

9   *In Matthaeum homilia* 12:6, PG 57:385.

10   Narsai of Nisibis, *Hom.* 17, ed. R. H. Connolly, *The Liturgical Homilies of Narsai* (Texts and Studies 8/1; Cambridge University Press, 1909), 8.

conform to the usage in the Ambrosian Rite,[11] but this seemed less desirable than having it in the first position.

The study group also expanded the number of options for the greeting. The first two forms in the current Missal are new greetings in the history of the liturgy, drawn from biblical texts. The second form originally came with a different response from the people. Instead of "And with your spirit" (or "And also with you," as the first English translation had it), the people had the option of responding, "Blessed be the God and Father of our Lord Jesus Christ."[12] The response of the people addressed God, not the priest. According to the study group, the dialogue "Grace and peace to you" and "Blessed be the God and Father" expressed the double reason of the entire liturgy, namely the grace of God, which descends from above, and the praise and prayer of the Church, which ascends to God.[13] However, this greeting and response were not much used, and the option, which appeared in an appendix in the first editions of the revised Missal, has been eliminated from the third edition.

The priest extends his hands while greeting the people. The rubrics say no more about how he should do this. Prior to the 1970 Missal, the priest extended his hands no wider than his body and no higher than his shoulder. The priest today is free to use a more natural gesture when addressing the people in his first greeting to them.

11 Braga, pp. 224 and 230.
12 2 Corinthians 1:3 and Ephesians 1:3.

13 Barba, p. 436.

Questions for Discussion and Reflection

1. Which greetings does the priest use for your community? Does the varying length of the greetings suggest varying degrees of solemnity?

_____

_____

_____

2. How do you understand the words, "And with your spirit"? How do they help you interpret the meaning of the greeting at the beginning of Mass?

_____

_____

_____

3. How does the priest extend his hands for the greeting? How natural is his gesture?

_____

_____

_____

4. Apart from the "Amen" that concludes the Sign of the Cross, these are the first words spoken between the priest and the people. How well are they establishing the purpose of this rite?

_____

_____

_____

5. Are any other words spoken before the Greeting? Does the cantor say anything? Does the priest say anything before giving the greeting? What effect does this have on the Introductory Rites of the liturgy?

INTRODUCTION TO THE MASS

3.　The Priest, or a Deacon, or another minister, may very briefly introduce the faithful to the Mass of the day.

Likewise it is also for the Priest, in the exercise of his office of presiding over the gathered assembly, to offer certain explanations that are foreseen in the rite itself. Where this is laid down by the rubrics, the celebrant is permitted to adapt them somewhat so that they correspond to the capacity for understanding of those participating. However, the Priest should always take care to keep to the sense of the explanatory text given in the Missal and to express it in just a few words. It is also for the presiding Priest to regulate the Word of God and to impart the final blessing. He is permitted, furthermore, in a very few words, to give the faithful an introduction to the Mass of the day (after the initial Greeting and before the Penitential Act), to the Liturgy of the Word (before the readings), and to the Eucharistic Prayer (before the Preface), though never during the Eucharistic Prayer itself; he may also make concluding comments regarding the entire sacred action before the Dismissal.

—GIRM, 31

See also GIRM, 48, 50, and 124.

Background

Study Group 10 inserted this introduction into the revised Missal; it had never existed before. Members believed that the active participation of the faithful could be assisted with appropriate catechesis, and this seemed like a good juncture to insert something. The introduction could explain parts of the Mass, or the nature of the celebration. The Introductory Rites were being simplified, and the people were being invited to make responses during them. An introduction by someone—priest, deacon or catechist—was permitted as an aid.

At first, the study group proposed putting the admonition after the words "Let us pray" and just before the text of the Collect. However, it was soon moved to its present position, after the greeting and before the Penitential Act.[1] This may explain why, in the previous English translation, the priest was permitted to expand the invitation to the Collect (Opening Prayer). For example, on the Sixth Sunday of Easter, he

---

1 Barba, p. 241.

could have said, "Let us pray that we may practice in our lives the faith we profess." Then silence followed before the priest continued with the text of the prayer: "Ever-living God, / help us to celebrate our joy / in the resurrection of the Lord / and to express in our lives / the love we celebrate." The revised English translation eliminates the option of "Let us pray for. . ." but retains the possibility of a brief introduction after the greeting.

Many worshipping communities have felt the need for words that personalize the gathering—acknowledging a wedding anniversary, introducing a catechumenate rite, announcing a special collection, or reporting local news of interest to the community. A carefully crafted introduction can meet this need within the context of the gathering of the people.

Questions for Discussion and Reflection

1. How often does someone give an introduction to the Mass?

_____

_____

_____

2. Who prepares the text? Who delivers it?

_____

_____

_____

3. How could your community use this option in an appropriate way?

_____

_____

_____

PENITENTIAL ACT*

4.   Then follows the Penitential Act, to which the Priest invites the faithful, saying:

Brethren (brothers and sisters), let us acknowledge
        our sins,
and so prepare ourselves to celebrate the sacred
        mysteries.

        A brief pause for silence follows. Then all recite together the formula of general confession:

I confess to almighty God
and to you, my brothers and sisters,
that I have greatly sinned,
in my thoughts and in my words,
in what I have done and in what I have failed to do,

        And, striking their breast, they say:

through my fault, through my fault,
through my most grievous fault;
        Then they continue:

therefore I ask blessed Mary ever-Virgin,
all the Angels and Saints,
and you, my brothers and sisters,
to pray for me to the Lord our God.

        The absolution by the Priest follows:

May almighty God have mercy on us,
forgive us our sins,
and bring us to everlasting life.

        The people reply:

Amen.

After this, the Priest calls upon the whole community to take part in the Penitential Act, which, after a brief pause for silence, it does by means of a formula of general confession. The rite concludes with the Priest's absolution, which, however, lacks the efficacy of the Sacrament of Penance.

From time to time on Sundays, especially in Easter Time, instead of the customary Penitential Act, the blessing and sprinkling of water may take place as a reminder of Baptism.

—GIRM, 51

See also GIRM, 40, 45, 125, 189, and 275a.

---

* From time to time on Sundays, especially in Easter Time, instead of the customary Penitential Act, the blessing and sprinkling of water may take place . . . as a reminder of Baptism.

Background

The heading for this next section, the Penitential Act, carries an asterisk to refer the reader to an appendix for the blessing and sprinkling of water. This has long been an option for Mass on Sunday. In the 1570 Missal, before Sunday Mass, the priest could exorcize and bless water in the sacristy, and then sprinkle the altar, himself, and the ministers. In the reform, this rite may replace the customary Penitential Act: the priest blesses the water in full view of the assembly, inviting their participation; he does not sprinkle the altar, but he does sprinkle himself, the ministers, and the people. All that remains of the exorcism (formerly addressed to the salt to be added to the water), is an optional blessing of salt, addressed to God.

Study Group 10 considered several options with the blessing and sprinkling of water: having it precede the principal Sunday Mass, moving it to the washing of the priest's hands, or eliminating it outside the Easter season and on major solemnities.[1] In the end, though, the members believed that the relegation of the rite to Sunday

Group 10, quoting more of a verse from the First Letter of John: "If we confess our sins, he who is faithful and just will forgive us our sins and cleanse us from all unrighteousness."[2]

The Confiteor used to be part of the prayers at the foot of the altar, which were abbreviated and rearranged to fit the new schema of Introductory Rites in the 1970 Missal. These elements appeared rather late in the development of the Eucharist. The first thousand years or so give scant evidence of a Penitential Act before the Collect. Saint Paul admonished the Corinthians to examine themselves before partaking in the supper.[3] Several decades later the *Didache* urged the faithful to confess their failings before the Sunday Eucharist.[4] A variety of private prayers for the priest were in use throughout the Middle Ages, but penitential formulas at the start of Mass were not fixed until the 1570 Missal. The priest recited the Confiteor, addressing God and the servers, and then the servers recited the Confiteor, addressing God and the priest.

The third edition of *The Roman Missal* expands the list of texts that may be sung during the sprinkling.

stresses its baptismal character, so it was incorporated into the Penitential Act as an optional replacement for its more penitential elements. This became more obvious by eliminating the sprinkling of the altar, and including that of the people.

Throughout the history of the rite, a separate text has been provided for the Easter season, under the presumption that water blessed at the Easter Vigil would be used again throughout the season for sprinklings and Baptisms. However, the Easter season text in the revised Missal still assumes that the water in question has not been blessed. The prayer is a blessing, and it is nearly identical to the one that blesses water at the Easter Vigil.

The third edition of *The Roman Missal* expands the list of texts that may be sung during the sprinkling. All this material appears in appendices to the book. The former English translation included the blessing and sprinkling of water within the Order of Mass, but it has always appeared in an appendix in Latin— even in the 1570 edition of the Missal.

The Penitential Act opens with an introduction from the priest. He invites the whole community—himself included—to acknowledge their sins. This is all that remains of a slightly longer formula proposed by Study

Even prior to 1570 the Confiteor existed, though the formula was not uniform. It always contained two parts: the acknowledgment of one's sin, and an appeal for intercession in obtaining forgiveness.[5] For the post-Vatican II revision of the Missal, Study Group 10 preferred the version already used by the Dominicans, which simplified the list of saints.[6]

The study group considered moving the entire Penitential Act to a different part of the Mass, for example as a bridge between the Liturgy of the Word and the Liturgy of the Eucharist, within the offertory, before Holy Communion, or even to a location subject to the judgment of the episcopal conferences.[7] The group also considered omitting the Penitential Act during the Easter season.[8] But the members eventually secured its position within the Introductory Rites.

The Confiteor assumed greater prominence in the 1970 Missal. It became one of several options, but most significantly the text, formerly

---

1   Barba, pp. 198–200, 213.

2   1 John 1:9. Barba, p. 217.

3   See 1 Corinthians 11:27–28.

4   *Didache* 14:1.

5   See Cabié, *The Church at Prayer*, 2:151.

6   Barba, p. 672.

7   Barba, p. 213.

8   Barba, p. 571.

recited by the priest alone and then by the servers, was shared now among the whole assembly.

The words have been simplified. In the 1570 Missal, the priest confessed to God, Mary, Saints Michael, John the Baptist, Peter and Paul, all the saints, and the community—mentioning the entire list twice, and striking his breast three times. In the revised text, God and Mary are mentioned by name, but the other names are subsumed into "all the Angels and Saints," and the word for "three times" has been removed at the instruction to strike one's breast—implying that the gesture is made once.

The previous English translation further simplified the text, reducing the threefold confession ("through my fault") to one, though that never had occurred in the Latin. The expression "most grievous fault," possibly an allusion to King David's confession of sin to God,[9] had also been retained in the Latin after the council, but it first appeared in English with the recently revised translation.

The prayer that follows the Confiteor is called "absolution," but from the beginning, the study group was concerned that the faithful not think it was the same as sacramental absolution.[10] Now that the texts would be said and heard in the vernacular, and now that the Confiteor would belong to the entire assembly, this became a concern.

The 1570 Missal had two prayers that could be called absolutions. The first appeared twice: when the priest finished his Confiteor, the servers said the absolution for him, and when the servers said their Confiteor, the priest said the

> Even prior to 1570 the Confiteor existed, though the formula was not uniform. It always contained two parts: the acknowledgment of one's sin, and an appeal for intercession in obtaining forgiveness.

absolution for them. Then the priest said a different prayer specifically asking for God's indulgence, absolution, and forgiveness.

In the reform of the Missal, after considering several options, the study group eventually eliminated the second prayer, and the first was assigned to the priest alone.[11] As the introduction to the Penitential Act invites everyone to acknowledge sins, and as the Confiteor expressed the sorrow of the entire community to the entire community, so the priest prays the absolution in the first person plural—asking for God's forgiveness upon all who have acknowledged sin together. To this, the people answer, "Amen."

---

9 See 1 Chronicles 21:8.
10 Barba, p. 214.

11 Barba, p. 223.

Questions for Discussion and Reflection

1. On what occasions does your worshipping community use the blessing and sprinkling of water? Why have you made those choices?

_____

_____

_____

2. How much silence is observed after the priest invites the community to recall its sins. Is it enough?

_____

_____

_____

3. When does your community opt to use the Confiteor? Have the faithful been instructed about the meaning of the words and the gesture?

_____

_____

_____

4. Does the absolution of the priest serve its purpose, inviting all to the hope of forgiveness and its rewards?

_____

_____

_____

5. The Priest invites the faithful to make the Penitential Act:

Brethren (brothers and sisters), let us acknowledge our sins,
and so prepare ourselves to celebrate the sacred mysteries.

A brief pause for silence follows.
The Priest then says:

Have mercy on us, O Lord.

The people reply:

For we have sinned against you.

The Priest:

Show us, O Lord, your mercy.

The people:

And grant us your salvation.

The absolution by the Priest follows:

May almighty God have mercy on us,
forgive us our sins,
and bring us to everlasting life.

The people reply:

Amen.

Background

The second option of the Penitential Act is based on verses of scripture.[1] However, its inspiration comes from the prayers at the foot of the altar from the 1570 Missal. In Study Group 10's original design, the priest invited people to penitence for their sins, using, as an example, both of the two lines that ultimately formed the first dialogue of this option. After a pause for silence, the next two lines were to be said in alternation between the priest and the people. These were taken directly from the prayers at the foot of the altar. This was the original option A, probably because of its resemblance to the prayers at the foot of the altar, but it became option B in the development of the Missal, probably to give more prominence to the Confiteor.[2]

The English translation for these lines changed considerably with the publication of the third edition of *The Roman Missal*, but the Latin text did not change. The 1970 English translation changed the first response of the people so that the first part of the dialogue appeared to be an abbreviated version of the Kyrie. In practice, the Kyrie that was intended to follow the second part was often omitted. In any case, this option has been little used by worshipping communities, though its brevity served the purposes of the Penitential Act and its context rather well. Although some elements of the Penitential Act may be led by other ministers, the priest leads this dialogue in its entirety.

---

1   See Baruch 3:2 and Psalm 84:8. In the Septuagint, the passage from Baruch calls God "Kyrie" and begs "eleison."
2   Barba, p. 216. The three options for the Penitential Act were originally given letters. The practice did not carry over into the Latin edition of the 1970 Missal, which placed the Confiteor in the Order of Mass, and the other two options in an appendix, labeling them 1 and 2. The first English translation, however, put all three options in the Order of Mass and assigned letters to them.

Questions for Discussion and Reflection

1. Has your community learned the responses to the second form of the Penitential Act?

2. On what occasions do you use it?

3. GIRM 40 suggests that dialogues be sung, and notes appear in the Missal for this form of the Penitential Act. When might your community sing it?

Or:

6.   The Priest invites the faithful to make the Penitential Act:

Brethren (brothers and sisters), let us acknowledge our sins,
and so prepare ourselves to celebrate the sacred mysteries.

A brief pause for silence follows.

The Priest, or a Deacon or another minister, then says
the following or other invocations with **Kyrie, eleison (Lord, have mercy):**

You were sent to heal the contrite of heart:
Lord, have mercy.   Or: Kyrie, eleison.

The people reply:

Lord, have mercy.   Or: Kyrie, eleison.

The Priest:

You came to call sinners.
Christ, have mercy. Or: Christe, eleison.

The people:

Christ, have mercy. Or: Christe, eleison.

The Priest:

You are seated at the right hand of the Father to intercede for us:
Lord, have mercy.   Or: Kyrie, eleison.

The people:

Lord, have mercy.   Or: Kyrie, eleison.

The absolution by the Priest follows:

May almighty God have mercy on us,
forgive us our sins,
and bring us to everlasting life.

The people reply:

Amen.

Background

The third option of the Penitential Act includes variable invocations addressed to Jesus as Lord or Christ. These may be delivered by any minister, and they may be freely composed.

It is thought that the Kyrie is all that remains of a longer processional litany that introduced the Eucharist.[1] When Study Group 10 created these invocations, its members attempted to restore something of the Kyrie's original form.[2] The study group first considered a structure similar to that of the second option, starting with the Kyrie and then using Psalm 103:10 as a dialogue, followed by a variable form of absolution.[3] It quickly settled, though, into the option known now. This structure had been proposed by French-speaking members of the group, and they chose invocations inspired by the Trisagion of the oriental liturgies: "Holy God, holy and strong God, holy and immortal God, Kyrie, eleison (repeated by all). You suffered for us on the cross. Christe, eleison. Remember us when you come into your kingdom. Kyrie, eleison."[4] These invocations eventually changed into those that now appear in the Missal, but in an appendix to the Order of Mass.[5] They have always retained the Greek words Kyrie, eleison and Christe, eleison at the close of each line. The first English translation abandoned this practice and concluded each invocation with the vernacular equivalent of the Greek formula. The third Latin edition moved this option from an appendix to a place within the Order of Mass, and the revised English translation offers both the vernacular and the Greek options for concluding each line.

Other invocations may be used. The first English translation gave a series of eight options, though the Latin editions have always offered only one. The English translation for that one still appears here in the Order of Mass, and the other have been moved to the appendix approved for use in the United States of America. Still, 'other' invocations may be used, so communities may compose their own in a similar style.

---

1   Peter Jeffrey, "The Meanings and Functions of *Kyrie eleison*," from *The Place of Christ in Liturgical Prayer: Trinity, Christology, and Liturgical Theology*, ed. Bryan D. Spinks (Collegeville, Minnesota: Liturgical Press, 2008):127–194.

2   Jeffrey disagrees with their solution.

3   Barba, p. 217.

4   Barba, p. 242.

---

5   They appear to be based on the following scripture passages: Psalm 147:3, Isaiah 61:1, Matthew 9:13, Romans 8:34, Ephesians 1:19–20, Colossians 3:1, Hebrews 1:3, and Hebrews 7:25.

Questions for Discussion and Reflection

1. How often do you use the third form of the Penitential Act in your worshipping community?

_____

_____

_____

2. Who composes the text?

_____

_____

_____

3. Who announces the invocations?

_____

_____

_____

4. How could the writing and speaking of these invocations be strengthened?

_____

_____

_____

5. On what occasions do you sing this form of the Penitential Act?

_____

_____

_____

KYRIE

7.   The Kyrie, eleison (Lord, have mercy) invocations follow, unless they have just occurred in a formula of the Penitential Act.

V. Lord, have mercy.   R. Lord, have mercy.

V. Christ, have mercy.   R. Christ, have mercy.

V. Lord, have mercy.   R. Lord, have mercy.

     Or:

V. Kyrie, eleison.   R. Kyrie, eleison.

V. Christe, eleison.   R. Christe, eleison.

V. Kyrie, eleison.   R. Kyrie, eleison.

After the Penitential Act, the *Kyrie, eleison* (Lord, have mercy), is always begun, unless it has already been part of the Penitential Act. Since it is a chant by which the faithful acclaim the Lord and implore his mercy, it is usually executed by everyone, that is to say, with the people and the choir or cantor taking part in it.

Each acclamation is usually pronounced twice, though it is not be excluded that it be repeated several times, by reason of the character of the various languages, as well as of the artistry of the music or of other circumstances. When the *Kyrie* is sung as a part of the Penitential Act, a "trope" precedes each acclamation.

—GIRM, 52

See also GIRM, 366.

Background

When Study Group 10 revised the Order of Mass, there was no question about retaining the Kyrie. One of the oldest parts of the Mass, it enjoyed a long tradition of musical accompaniment, and it could serve the overall goal of enhancing the participation of the people.[1]

The origins of the Kyrie are not clear. The word "eleison" has pre-Christian roots in Homer, where people in great distress appealed for help to someone whose decisions they could not control.[2] It was unrelated to repentance. Saint Paul applied the role "Lord" to Christ,[3] possibly to usurp the title of an incumbent earthly ruler; Christians use the same word for any member of the Trinity—it is not reserved to Christ.

Egeria says she heard "Kyrie, eleison" in Jerusalem in the late fourth century, where it served as an intercessory refrain following the singing of Psalms and a procession.[4] In Gaul the Council of Vaison (529) called for the repetition of the Kyrie at "matins, masses and vespers," though it did not specify what function it served at Mass.[5] Gregory the Great probably set the Kyrie firmly near the beginning of the Mass as part of his many reforms.[6] It clearly appears before the Gloria in *Ordo Romanus I*.[7] One theory is that it occupied this place because of its connection to processional litanies, notably the litany of the saints.[8] Originally the word "Kyrie" was probably addressed to God, not necessarily to Christ, and "eleison" was a general cry for

---

1   Barba, pp. 223, 226.

2   *Iliad* 21:74; 22:59, 82; 24:503; *Odyssey* 22:312, 344; see Jeffrey, p. 144.

3   See Romans 10:9; 1 Corinthians 12:3; Philippians 2:11.

4   *Diary of Egeria* 24:5. Wilkinson, p. 143.

5   Canon 3, CCL 148A:79.

6   Epistle 9, PL 77:955-958.

7   OR I:52.

8   Jeffrey, pp. 177–190.

mercy, not a specific appeal for forgiveness. Because the Septuagint used "Kyrios" for the holy name of God in the Old Testament, and Paul had applied the same title to Christ, the Kyrie logically adopted its "Christe, eleison" petition. Although the unit originated as a dialogue with the people, the Kyrie in the Middle Ages was sung by the choir alone.

Consequently Study Group 10 was anxious to restore the Kyrie to the participation of the people in revised Introductory Rites. However, the members understood its function to serve an interior penitential discipline of the newly gathered assembly, rather than the conclusion of processional music preceding the greeting. Still, questions were raised. If the Prayer of the Faithful was being restored, might the Kyrie be a useless duplication to be completely removed from the Mass?[9] It was even recommended that the Kyrie

be eliminated at Masses in which the Gloria would be sung.[10] However, Pope Paul VI personally desired the retention of the Kyrie in some way.[11] The only change in its form was the reduction from three sets of three petitions each, to three sets of two, which ameliorated their dialogic function. It is still permissible to sing the Kyrie in three sets of threes, especially when using one of the traditional chants.

The Kyrie is omitted only when the third option of the Penitential Act is used. In this

> Originally the word "Kyrie" was probably addressed to God, not necessarily to Christ, and "eleison" was a general cry for mercy, not a specific appeal for forgiveness.

case, however, it is more accurate to say it is absorbed into the third option. Hence the Kyrie is still used in all Masses, with any option of the Penitential Act.

---

9 Barba, p. 437.

10 Ibid.

11 Barba, p. 229.

Questions for Discussion and Reflection

1. In your community, when do you sing the Kyrie?

_____

_____

_____

2. Do you ever use the Greek words instead of the English ones?

_____

_____

_____

3. Is the Kyrie part of every Mass in some form?

_____

_____

_____

GLORIA

8.   Then, when it is prescribed, this hymn is either sung or said:

Glory to God in the highest,
and on earth peace to people of good will.

We praise you,
we bless you,
we adore you,
we glorify you,
we give you thanks for your great glory,
Lord God, heavenly King,
O God, almighty Father.

Lord Jesus Christ, Only Begotten Son,
Lord God, Lamb of God, Son of the Father,
you take away the sins of the world,
        have mercy on us;
you take away the sins of the world,
        receive our prayer;
you are seated at the right hand of the Father,
        have mercy on us.

For you alone are the Holy One,
you alone are the Lord,
you alone are the Most High,
Jesus Christ,
with the Holy Spirit,
in the glory of God the Father.
Amen.

The *Gloria in excelsis* (*Glory to God in the highest*) is a most ancient and venerable hymn by which the Church, gathered in the Holy Spirit, glorifies and entreats God the Father and the Lamb. . . .

—GIRM, 53

See also GIRM, 126, and 275a.

Background

The Introductory Rites take on a celebratory character on the occasions when the Gloria is sung. It is prescribed for Sundays outside of Advent and Lent, and it is omitted on th erare instances when All Souls Day falls on a Sunday. It is used for solemnities and feasts on the calendar, and it is appropriate for "special celebrations of a more solemn character."[1] These need not, but could include ordinations, weddings and confirmations.

The text probably comes from the Oriental Churches. The fourth century *Apostolic Constitutions*, an early church order governing prayer and behavior, include a version of it as a daily morning prayer, detached from any celebration of the Eucharist.[2] The *Liber Pontificalis*, a book containing biographies of the popes, says that Pope Symmachus (+514) called for the Gloria to

---

1   Ibid.

2   AC 7:47. A disputed work of Athanasius also gives the opening verses, "*De Virginitate*" 20, PG 28:275.

be sung on every Sunday and feast of the martyrs.[3] The *Gregorian Sacramentary*, compiled by the seventh or eighth century from papal liturgies, gives the first clear witness that the Gloria should be sung at Mass when the Bishop is present on Sundays and feasts. It could not be sung in his absence at Masses with presbyters, except at Easter.[4] The first line of the hymn comes from the Gospel account of the birth of Jesus,[5] so many have deduced that the hymn has its origins in Christmas celebrations. But the rest of the text could just as easily pertain to the Easter season, when its use was more extensive.[6] In *Ordo Romanus I*, the litanies that accompanied the Kyrie came to a close when the Bishop intoned the Gloria.[7] In the 1570 Missal the Gloria followed the Kyrie, and the greeting followed the Gloria. The Missal included the musical notes for the priest to intone the Gloria, but if the choir sang the rest of the text, he recited it himself privately. If the music took some time, he and the assembly may have sat down until the choir finished. While reciting the Gloria, the priest was instructed to bow his head at four different phrases, and to sign himself with the cross at the end. The Gloria was not sung at every Mass, but at quite a number of them.

The GIRM for the 1970 Missal reduced the occasions on which to include the Gloria. This made the Introductory Rites more festive on those days, and more focused when it was omitted. Prior to 2002, the revised Missal gave no specific instructions about who began the Gloria.[8] It seemed fitting for all to begin it together, especially if it were sung. However, the priest often started the recited text out of practicality. The 2002 GIRM now explicitly states that the Gloria "is intoned by the Priest or, if appropriate, by a cantor or by the choir."[9] The Order of Mass now includes the notes for the priest to sing. Although the text in the first line does not require a priest any more than the rest of the hymn does, the tradition for the presider to start the Gloria reaches back a long time. It probably originated as a way for the Bishop, concluding his Entrance Procession, to raise his voice first in praise of God before greeting the people, and out of a practical need for someone to start this part of the Mass.

Even though the Gloria would be used less frequently, Study Group 10 still labored to unify the disparate elements of the Introductory Rites. The members considered moving the Gloria to a place after the Collect or even following the Prayer after Communion.[10] They also thought the greeting belonged earlier.

In the end, the Gloria kept its traditional place after the Kyrie, the occasions for its use were reduced, and the greeting moved forward where it served as the first words exchanged between the priest and the people.

No rules govern when the Gloria should be sung or recited. Individual worshipping communities have established their own patterns; for example, by reciting it during Ordinary Time Sundays, but singing it on other occasions. Although the traditional chant melodies of the Gloria contributed to its festive nature, many contemporary settings have used rhythm to engage a stronger emotional response from worshippers.

---

3   LP I:263.

4   *Le Sacramentaire Grégorien* 2.

5   See Luke 2:14.

6   Stefano Parenti, "*Lo studio e la storia della messa Romana nella prespettiva della liturgia comparata: Alcuni esempi*," *Ecclesia Orans* 25/2 (Maggio-Agosto 2008): pp. 209–210.

7   OR I:53.

8   See the pre-2002 GIRM, 31.

9   GIRM, 53.

10 Barba, p. 224.

Questions for Discussion and Reflection

1. In your worshipping community, who intones the Gloria?

_____

_____

_____

2. When do you sing it and recite it? Why?

_____

_____

_____

3. Does your worshipping community have more than one sung setting of the Gloria in repertoire? How do you decide which to use?

_____

_____

_____

COLLECT

9.   When this hymn is concluded, the Priest, with hands joined, says:

Let us pray.

And all pray in silence with the Priest for a while.

Then the Priest, with hands extended, says the Collect prayer, at the end of which the people acclaim:

Amen.

Next the Priest calls upon the people to pray and everybody, together with the Priest, observes a brief silence so that they may become aware of being in God's presence and may call to mind their intentions. Then the Priest pronounces the prayer usually called the "Collect" and through which the character of the celebration finds expression. . . .

—GIRM, 54

See also GIRM, 32, 40, 45, 127, and 189.

Background

The invitation, "Let us pray," leads everyone into a period of silence, during which they formulate the prayers they bring to Mass this day. The priest gathers the prayer of the assembly into one, addressing a formal, structured, and—often—very ancient text to God. The people answer, "Amen."

The whole formula is called the Collect. Formerly known as the Opening Prayer, it brings the Introductory Rites to their logical conclusion as the assembly that has gathered in song, signed itself with the cross, greeted one another, acknowledged individual faults, and praised God, now gets down to business. On behalf of the people, the priest addresses to God words pertaining to the particular celebration now underway.

The word "Collect" may have originally referred to the gathering of the people, rather than the gathering of their prayer. It was the prayer offered upon everyone's arrival.[1] Ample examples of the texts can be found as early as the sixth century _Veronese Sacramentary_, which first gathered the burgeoning composition of prayers for Mass in Rome, and assigned a suite of prayers for specific days. In many cases, these prayers are original versions of ones that appear in _The Roman Missal_.

A traditional Roman Collect is carefully constructed. It contains an invocation that names God, a phrase that amplifies who God is or what God has done, a petition that names the request, a purpose that expresses the goal of the request, a motive that clarifies the reasonableness of the petition, and a concluding doxolo-

---

1   Adrian Fortescue, _The Mass: A Study of the Roman Liturgy,_ (London, England: Longmans, Green and Co., 1950), pp. 244–245.

gy.[2] These elements intertwine, so that, for example, the phrase that expresses God's good deeds may set up the theme for the petition.

The phrase, "Let us pray," is quite ancient and even has roots in pre-Christian Jewish prayer.[3] It appears in liturgical texts in *Ordo Romanus I*.[4] It does not presume that no prayer has happened up to now, any more than the same phrase after Communion does. It announces the purpose of what follows.

The silence following this invitation is integral to its purpose. During the silence the faithful are to formulate in their hearts the prayers they hold this day, the prayers they bring to this Mass. They will have more opportunities for this, but in the Introductory Rites, they make this particular celebration their own. Silence is new to the Vatican II Missal.

The doxology makes the prayer to the Father, through Christ, in the Holy Spirit. It embeds a Christological affirmation, though this is difficult to hear in the English translation. The prayer is addressed to the Father "through Jesus Christ—God—who lives and reigns with you in the unity of the Holy Spirit." Grammatically, the word "God" refers to Jesus.

The word "Amen" appears throughout the Bible.[5] The Hebrew word has always been so clearly understood that it defied translation in ancient and modern languages. Revelation 3:14 treats "Amen" as the name for Jesus, and in John 15:16 Jesus said the Father would grant

> A traditional Roman Collect is carefully constructed. It contains an invocation that names God, a phrase that amplifies who God is or what God has done, a petition that names the request, a purpose that expresses the goal of the request, a motive that clarifies the reasonableness of the petition, and a concluding doxology.

whatever the disciples ask in his name. When the people answer "Amen" to the Collect, they are saying "yes" to its contents, but they are also pronouncing the name of him through whom they pray God will grant their request.

The GIRM says pointedly that only one Collect is to be said.[6] In the 1570 Missal it was common to use more than one. The reform of the Missal limited the number of collects to illuminate the purpose of the prayer. The revised Missal made the Collect more accessible to the people: It introduced a period of silent prayer and handed over the "Amen." Accented by the use of the vernacular, the Collect became the prayer not just of the priest, but of the entire assembly, praising God, and making its intentions known on high.

---

2   See *Appreciating the Collect: An Irenic Methodology,* ed. James. G. Leachman and Daniel P McCarthy (Farnborough, United Kingdom: Saint Michael's Abbey, 2008), p. 75.

3   Klauser, p. 6.

4   OR I:53.

---

5   Examples are many, but a few can be found in Numbers 5:22, Deuteronomy 27:15–26, Jeremiah 11:5, Nehemiah 5:13, and Psalms 41:13; 72:19; 89:52; 106:48. Among the examples in the New Testament are Revelation 1:6, 3:14, and 7:12.

6   See GIRM, 54.

Questions for Discussion and Reflection

1. In your community, how well observed is the silence that follows the words "Let us pray"?

_____

_____

_____

2. How well is the assembly using the silence it receives?

_____

_____

_____

3. Who holds the book for the priest while he says this prayer? Is that minister in place before the words, "Let us pray," or does the movement of the minister fill the silence?

_____

_____

_____

4. How well do the people understand the words of the Collect as the priest says them?

_____

_____

_____

5. On what occasions does the priest sing the Collect?

_____

_____

_____

6. How strong is the "Amen" of the people? Do some members of the assembly take their seats before saying, "Amen," in anticipation of the next part of the Mass?

_____

_____

_____

7. How would you describe the arc of the Introductory Rites as they are celebrated in your worshipping community? What are the high points? Why? What should the high points be? Why?

_____

_____

_____

THE LITURGY
OF THE WORD

FIRST READING

10.   Then the reader goes to the ambo and reads the First Reading, while all sit and listen.

     To indicate the end of the reading, the reader acclaims:

The word of the Lord.

     All reply:

Thanks be to God.

. . . For in the readings, as explained by the Homily, God speaks to his people, opening up to them the mystery of redemption and salvation, and offering spiritual nourishment; and Christ himself is present through his word in the midst of the faithful. By silence and by singing, the people make this divine word their own, and affirm their adherence to it by means of the Profession of Faith; finally, having been nourished by the divine word, the people pour out their petitions by means of the Universal Prayer for the needs of the whole Church and for the salvation of the whole world.

—GIRM, 55

See also GIRM, 29, 31, 40, 43, 45, 56, 57, 58, 59, 128, 130, 171df, 176, 196, 309, 339, and 362; and *Lectionary for Mass* (LM), 14, 15, 16, 28, 38, 42, and 46.

Background

The readings from sacred scripture form the community in its weekly gathering. One of the greatest contributions the Second Vatican Council made to Catholic worship was the revision of the *Lectionary for Mass*. People started hearing more scripture than ever before. The number of Sunday readings increased from two to three, and the brief Psalm verse known as the gradual expanded into the richer Responsorial Psalm. The one-year cycle of readings expanded to a three-year cycle. Formerly, Catholics heard 1% of the Old Testament and 17% of the New Testament. Now they hear 14% of the Old Testament and 71% of the New Testament. The readings are arranged within a sensible framework from week to week and season to season. The interplay of thematic materials makes them useful for preaching and catechesis. By separating the Missal into two books—one for prayers and the other for readings—the Council not only made a practical decision to accommodate the increase in texts, but it restored the practice whereby the readings appeared in a separate volume, distinct from other parts of the Mass because they are the word of God.

The two-part service (Word and Eucharist) evolved from patterns of Jewish worship.[1] It almost certainly lies behind Luke's account of the journey to Emmaus,[2] in which two disciples converse unawares with Jesus on the evening of the day he rose from the dead. Along the way, he explains the prophetic scriptures to them. Then, when he breaks the bread, they recognize who he is. This Word-and-Eucharist framework existed from the very beginnings of Christian worship.

Proclaiming the scriptures aloud expresses their original design. The Bible was written for public proclamation, not just for private devotion. The New Testament itself reports the practice of reading and hearing apostolic writings to Christian communities.[3]

In the middle of the second century, the reading of scripture was already a fixed part of the Sunday gathering. Justin the Martyr implies that no other ceremonies preceded it.

     On the day we call the day of the sun, all who dwell in the city or country gather in the same place.

1   Klauser, p. 5.
2   See Luke 24:13–35.
3   See Colossians 4:16; Philemon 2; Revelation 1:3.

The memoirs of the apostles and the writings of the prophets are read, as much as time permits.

~~When the reader has finished, he who~~ presides over those gathered admonishes and challenges them to imitate these beautiful things.[4]

A few decades later, Tertullian wrote of hearing in North Africa the law and the prophets with the Gospel and apostolic letters.[5] By the fourth century, Ambrose of Milan knew the basic sequence of readings that has become so familiar. He wrote, "first the prophet is read, and the apostle and then the gospel"[6]—though the setting may not have been the Eucharist. Many early Christian basilicas were designed with twin ambos for the proclamation of the epistle (on the liturgical south side) and the Gospel (on the north). The separation of the ambos indicated the distinction that should be accorded the Gospel, which was proclaimed from the north as if evangelization needed to happen to the geographically southern part of the world.[7] In places without two separate ambos, the epistle would be read from the lower step of the ambo, again to give the Gospel its distinction.

By the Middle Ages the public reading of the scriptures from ambos had been abandoned. The celebrant and ministers read the texts in Latin in a low voice. The epistle was read from the right side of the altar (its liturgical south side), and—on ordinary occasions when the priest presided without the deacon—he then moved the Missal to the left side for the Gospel. He turned the book slightly, in remembrance of an earlier custom when he actually read to the people, and continued reading in a low voice.[8]

In 1960, after the Second Vatican Council had been announced but not yet convened, Pope John XXIII issued a clarification of the rubrics for the Mass. He asked that the readings all be proclaimed in a clear voice.[9] By this time it was becoming customary for people to hear the scriptures in the vernacular, but the ministers still read the same passages quietly in Latin.

Today the reader should be someone other than the priest or the deacon, but they may perform the function if necessary. The readings should be proclaimed from the ambo, which is reserved for the key elements of the Liturgy of the Word. The assembly, which has been standing, changes its posture and sits. However, the

> The readings should be proclaimed from the ambo, which is reserved for the key elements of the Liturgy of the Word.

Order of Mass clarifies that the people do not merely sit. They "sit and listen."

Many worshipping communities provide printed copies of the readings for all to follow. This was never envisioned by the rubrics and is not encouraged. Although some other Christian denominations promote bringing a Bible to church in order to follow the proclaimed readings, Catholic piety has developed around a different value. God speaks to the people in the proclamation of the Word, not in the common silent reading of the Word; and Christ speaks to the people—in the present tense—whenever the Gospel is proclaimed.

The reader's acclamation at the conclusion, and the people's reply first appeared in the 1970 Missal, but they are not foreign to the Christian tradition. This brief dialogue announces and acknowledges that the reading has come to its conclusion. However, the words are given a spiritual tone, as the people express their thanks to God for the proclamation of the divine Word.

---

4   Justin, *Apology* I:65-67. Cited in CCC, 1345.

5   *De Praescriptione haereticorvm* 36:3, CCL 1:217.

6   Ambrose, *In Psalmum David CXVIII Expositio* 17, 10, PL 15:1443; translation PT.

7   Cabié, *The Church at Prayer* 2:152.

8   Klauser, p. 104.

---

9   *Codex rubricarum*, 511. Cf. http://www.ceremoniaire. net/print/pastorale1950/Rubriques-1960.pdf.

Questions for Discussion and Reflection

1. Who assumes the ministry of reader in your worshipping community? How are these persons chosen? How are they trained?

_____

_____

_____

2. Is the ambo reserved for the Liturgy of the Word in your church? Or is it used for other functions as well? Who speaks from the ambo and why?

_____

_____

_____

3. Where do you store the volumes of the Lectionary between Masses? Is that a worthy place for the word of God?

_____

_____

_____

4. Do the people follow the scriptures from printed matter with their eyes or from the reader with their ears? Why?

_____

_____

_____

5. Are the other ministers in the sanctuary attentive to the scriptures as they are proclaimed? How do they show their participation?

_____

_____

_____

RESPONSORIAL PSALM

11.	The psalmist or cantor sings or says the Psalm, with the people making the response.

After the First Reading follows the Responsorial Psalm, which is an integral part of the Liturgy of the Word and which has great liturgical and pastoral importance, since it fosters meditation on the Word of God. . . .

It is preferable for the Responsorial Psalm to be sung, at least as far as the people's response is concerned. . . .

—GIRM, 61

See also GIRM, 57, 63, 99, 102, 105b, 129, 196, 309, 312, and 352.

Background

The Psalm that follows the First Reading is "responsorial" because of its form, not because of its function. It is designed to be sung in alternation between the psalmist and the people; thus, making it responsorial. Although it usually echoes a theme from the First Reading, it is not a "response" to the reading. On rare occasions, the Psalm is chosen because it is cited in the Gospel of the day, or even because of a motif in the Second Reading.

The singing of Psalms with readings from scripture at Christian worship is mentioned by Tertullian.[1] Augustine preached on the Psalms, elevating their status among the proclaimed readings. "The Psalm that we have just heard sung, and to which we have responded by singing, is short, and very profitable."[2] By the eighth century, *Ordo Romanus I* says that after the reading the cantor ascends the ambo and sings a "response."[3] The *Gregorian Sacramentary* calls it the "gradual,"[4] probably because it was sung from the lower part of the ambo, up one step or "grade" from ground level. As the Gregorian chant tradition developed, the gradual lost its responsorial nature. It most commonly consisted of two verses of a Psalm; only the second one was called a "verse," and that was all that remained of its original function. During Easter, the first line was replaced with an Alleluia.

In the current rite, both the GIRM and the Order of Mass use the word "psalmist" for the one who sings the Psalm. The word had disappeared from the liturgy over the years, but was restored after the Council. In many worshipping communities, the cantor or song leader is also the psalmist. But the unique usage of the word for this part of the Mass indicates a special role, as well as the significance of the Psalm.

The Psalm may be sung from any suitable place, but the ambo is recommended because its text comes from sacred scripture.[5]

1	Tertullian, *De anima* 9:4, CCL 2:792.
2	Augustine, *Ennarationes in Psalmos* 119:1, CCL 40:1776; translation PT.
3	OR I:57; translation PT.
4	*Le Sacramentaire Grégorien*, 2; translation PT.
5	See GIRM, 309.

Questions for Discussion and Reflection

1. Who leads the Responsorial Psalm? Is it usually sung? How is the psalmist trained?

2. From where is the Psalm sung? From the ambo or another suitable place? Why?

_____

_____

_____

3. How often in the liturgical year does the homilist refer to the Psalm?

_____

_____

_____

4. Who manages the silence between the First Reading and the Responsorial Psalm? Does everyone—including the musicians—honor the silence?

_____

_____

_____

SECOND READING

12.   After this, if there is to be a Second Reading, a reader reads it from the ambo, as above.

To indicate the end of the reading, the reader acclaims:

The word of the Lord.

All reply:

Thanks be to God.

If there is to be a Second Reading before the Gospel, the reader proclaims it from the ambo. All listen and at the end reply to the acclamation, as noted above (no. 128). Then, if appropriate, a few moments of silence may be observed.

—GIRM, 130

See also GIRM, 128.

Background

The weekly proclamation of a Second Reading before the Gospel is a much appreciated contribution of the 1970 Missal. However, there is evidence for multiple readings in some earlier sources. The late fourth century *Apostolic Constitutions*, for example, calls for a lengthy word service:

> In the middle, let the reader stand upon some high place: let him read the books of Moses, of Joshua the son of Nun, of the Judges, and of the Kings and of the Chronicles, and those written after the return from the captivity; and besides these, the books of Job and of Solomon, and of the sixteen prophets But when there have been two lessons severally read, let some other person sing the hymns of David, and let the people join at the conclusions of the verses. Afterwards let our Acts be read, and the Epistles of Paul our fellow-worker, which he sent to the churches under the conduct of the Holy Spirit; and afterwards let a deacon or a presbyter read the Gospels.[1]

---

1   AC 2:57, 5–9; *Ante-Nicene Fathers*, Second Printing, ed. Alexander Roberts and James Donaldson (Peabody, Massachusettes: Hendrickson Publishers, Inc., 1995) 7:421.

Questions for Discussion and Reflection

1. How does the second reader enter the sanctuary for the reading? Do the reader and the psalmist need to exchange places? How smoothly does this happen?

_____

_____

_____

2. How well is silence observed after the Second Reading? Does the reader leave the ambo immediately or remain in place a few moments? Why?

_____

_____

_____

3. Does the second reader put away the Lectionary so that the *Book of the Gospel*s can be brought to the ambo unencumbered? If so, where does the Lectionary go? Does this take place during the silence or after it? Why?

_____

_____

_____

GOSPEL ACCLAMATION

13.   There follows the **Alleluia** or another chant laid down by the rubrics, as the liturgical time requires.

> After the reading that immediately precedes the Gospel, the *Alleluia* or another chant laid down by the rubrics is sung, as the liturgical time requires. An acclamation of this kind constitutes a rite or act in itself, by which the gathering of the faithful welcome and greets the Lord who is about to speak to them in the Gospel and profess their faith by means of the chant. It is sung by everybody, standing, and is led by the choir or a cantor, being repeated as the case requires. The verse, on the other hand, is sung either by the choir or by a cantor. . . .
>
> —GIRM, 62
>
> See also GIRM, 45, 62, 63c, 64, 130, and 309.

Background

This acclamation announces the coming of the Gospel and accompanies the procession to the ambo. It may be omitted if it is not sung.[1] The Order of Mass says the Alleluia or "another chant" follows the Second Reading. The other chant is a reference to the acclamation that replaces the Alleluia during Lent, but it also refers to the singing of the Sequence.

---

1   GIRM, 63c.

If there is a Sequence, it precedes the Alleluia. There are four Sequences in the Lectionary. The ones for the solemnities of Easter Sunday and Pentecost are obligatory (the Sequence for Easter Sunday is optional throughout the octave of Easter), but those for the solemnity of the Most Holy Body and Blood of Christ and for the memorial of Our Lady of Sorrows are optional. Sequences were popular throughout the Middle Ages, and quite a number of them prevailed throughout the liturgical year.[2] They served the function that many of our hymns do today, except that people sang them right during the Liturgy of the Word. In an earlier tradition, the Sequence *followed* the Alleluia; when the revised GIRM was first published in the year 2000, it retained that tradition, even though these elements had been reversed in practice. The 2002 GIRM corrected the current order of the chants: The Sequence comes first so that the Alleluia retains its purpose to announce the Gospel.

The Hebrew word "Alleluia" means "Praise God." Its origins in liturgical worship are quite ancient. It appears several times in the Book of Psalms as a shout of joy,[3] and only once in the New Testament, in the Book of Revelation, where it serves as a refrain for a hymn sung to the Lamb, the risen Christ.[4]

Perhaps this is why the Alleluia became attached to the season of Easter. Sozomen (+450) says it was sung only on Easter Day in Rome.[5] The acclamation was in use in various Eastern rites.[6] Gregory the Great criticized John of Syracuse for singing the Alleluia outside the fifty days of the season.[7] *Ordo Romanus I* has the cantor sing Alleluia "in season," and the tract otherwise.[8] It is followed by the Gospel.

In chant the opening notes of the Alleluia were sung by the cantor, and then the schola repeated them and finished the line. After a verse, the Alleluia was sung again—the cantor singing the first notes, and the schola singing the rest.

The tract was a chant that differed in text and structure. Of course it omitted the word "Alleluia," but it was also sung straight through without the repetition of one of its parts; that is, it was sung as a single tract; hence, its name.[9]

---

2   Oury, p. 82.
3   See, for example, Psalms 113—119 and 146—150.

4   See Revelation 19:1–6.
5   *Historia Ecclesiastica* 7:19, PG 67, 1475–1476.
6   Jungmann 1:423.
7   PL 77:956, Letter 9.
8   OR I:57.
9   Fortiscue, p. 271, citing Amalarius of Metz *De ecclesiasticis officiis libri iv*, 3:12, PL 105:1121, where he distinguishes between the responsory and the tract as the songs of two different kinds of birds—one enjoying melodious company, the other not.

Questions for Discussion and Reflection

1. Has your community learned musical settings of the Sequences for Easter and Pentecost? Are they sung each year?

_____

_____

_____

2. How do you handle the other two Sequences?

_____

_____

_____

3. Is the Gospel Acclamation sung at every Mass? Do you omit it if it is not sung?

_____

_____

_____

4. Has the community learned a variety of musical settings for the Gospel Acclamations? What do you sing during the season of Lent?

_____

_____

_____

5. Who gives the cue to begin the music for the Gospel Acclamation? The priest? The deacon? The musicians? Why?

_____

_____

_____

GOSPEL

14.   Meanwhile, if incense is used, the Priest puts some into the thurible. After this, the Deacon who is to proclaim the Gospel, bowing profoundly before the Priest, asks for the blessing, saying in a low voice:

Your blessing, Father.

The Priest says in a low voice:

May the Lord be in your heart and on your lips
that you may proclaim his Gospel worthily and well,
in the name of the Father and of the Son ✠ and of the
    Holy Spirit.

The Deacon signs himself with the Sign of the Cross and replies:

Amen.

If, however, a Deacon is not present, the Priest, bowing before the altar, says quietly:

Cleanse my heart and my lips, almighty God,
that I may worthily proclaim your holy Gospel.

During the singing of the *Alleluia* or other chant, if incense is being used, the Deacon ministers to the Priest as he puts incense into the thurible. Then, bowing profoundly before the Priest, he asks for the blessing, saying in a low voice, *Your blessing, Father. . . .*

—GIRM, 175

See also GIRM, 59 and 275b.

Background

Before proclaiming the Gospel, a deacon goes to the priest for a blessing. If the Bishop presides at a Mass with concelebrants but without deacons, the priest who reads the Gospel asks the Bishop for the blessing. But a priest does not ask another priest for the blessing. He says the same formula the celebrant says when he reads the Gospel in the absence of a deacon. In doing so, he makes a profound bow to the altar.

In *Ordo Romanus I*, the deacon approached the Bishop before proclaiming the Gospel. The Bishop simply said to him, "May the Lord be in your heart and on your lips." There is some early evidence for him signing the deacon with the cross, but that likely developed later.[1] Various private prayers were said by the priest and the deacon at key points during the Mass,[2] and the ones for the proclamation of the Gospel appear to be settled with the publication of the 1474 Missal. In the 1570 Missal, the custom appears the way it is today: a deacon asked the priest for a blessing, which he then gave; a priest reciting the Gospel offered the prayer privately for himself.

The innovation to the rubrics in the 2002 GIRM may simply be a clarification: the deacon signs himself with the cross while the priest says the blessing.

1   OR I:59.
2   Oury, p. 82.

Questions for Discussion and Reflection

1. Where do the priest and deacon stand for their conversation? What postures do they assume?

_____

_____

_____

2. If the priest proclaims the Gospel, where does he recite this text? What posture does he assume?

_____

_____

_____

3. Are the words indeed said quietly? Why is this important? Are the postures and gestures visible? Is that important?

_____

_____

_____

15.   The Deacon, or the Priest, then proceeds to the ambo, accompanied, if appropriate, by ministers with incense and candles. There he says:

The Lord be with you.

The people reply:

And with your spirit.

The Deacon, or the Priest:

A reading from the holy Gospel according to N.

and, at the same time, he makes the Sign of the Cross on the book and on his forehead, lips, and breast.

The reading of the Gospel constitutes the high point of the Liturgy of the Word. The Liturgy itself teaches the great reverence that is to be shown to this reading by setting it off from the other readings with special marks of honor, by the fact of which minister is appointed to proclaim it and by the blessing or prayer with which he prepares himself; and also by the fact that through their acclamations the faithful acknowledge and confess that Christ is present and is speaking to them and stand as they listen to the reading; and by the mere fact of the marks of reverence that are given to the Book of Gospels.

—GIRM, 60

See also GIRM, 29, 33, 40, 43, 59, 131, 132, 133, 134, 175, 273, 275b, 276c, and 277.

The people acclaim:

Glory to you, O Lord.

Then the Deacon, or the Priest, incenses the book, if incense is used, and proclaims the Gospel.

Background

Several marks of respect are given the Gospel. The *Book of the Gospels* may be carried in procession from the altar to the ambo. Candles and incense may lead the way. The people stand. The Gospel Acclamation is sung. An ordained minister prepares himself for the proclamation. He greets the people; they respond. The Gospel is announced and the Sign of the Cross is made over the book, the forehead, lips, and breast. The people respond, making similar gestures. The book may be incensed. Finally, the Gospel is proclaimed. A rich panoply of symbols unspools in rapid, smooth succession. The liturgy makes every effort to show how important this moment is.

The designation of a special minister for reading the Gospel goes all the way back to the third century. Cyprian (+258) ordained Aurelian for this purpose.[1] A century later Sozomen said a Bishop read the Gospel at Easter in Constantinople, and an archdeacon read it in Alexandria, and in many other churches it was proclaimed by a deacon or a presbyter.[2]

The use of candles and incense is in evidence by *Ordo Romanus I*.[3] They appeared at a time in history when the growth of vernacular languages meant the Latin texts of the Mass were less understood. Ritual elements increased to help convey meaning.[4] The greeting of the people, the announcement of the evangelist, and the signs of the cross appeared in the 1570 Missal and are still in force today.

The designation of a special minister for reading the Gospel goes all the way back to the third century.

At first, the Gospel was proclaimed from an ambo on the liturgical north side of the building, but in time it was read from the altar from the same book used for other prayers at the Mass. To show the distinction, the book was moved from the right to the left side of the altar.[5]

The 2002 GIRM has confirmed a custom that had already been widely practiced. The people sign themselves on the forehead lips and breast as the priest or deacon does. They did so prior to 2002, but no rubric called for it.

---

1 *Epistola* 33, PL 4:319.
2 *Historia ecclesiastica* 7:19, PG 67:1477–1478.

3 OR I:59.
4 Oury, p. 81.
5 *Micrologus de ecclesiasticis observationibus* 9, PL 151:982.

Questions for Discussion and Reflection

1. On what occasions does your community use incense for the Gospel?

_____

_____

_____

2. On what occasions do you have a procession with candles?

_____

_____

_____

3. Do you use the *Book of the Gospels*? Is it resting on the altar before the procession begins?

_____

_____

_____

4. What is the path of the procession? Does it move smoothly?

_____

_____

_____

5. Is the Gospel ever sung? When and why then?

_____

_____

_____

6. How does your community experience the special nature of the proclamation of the Gospel?

_____

_____

_____

16.   At the end of the Gospel, the Deacon, or the Priest, acclaims:

The Gospel of the Lord.

All reply:

Praise to you, Lord Jesus Christ.

Then he kisses the book, saying quietly:

Through the words of the Gospel may our sins be wiped away.

. . . Lastly, the deacon may carry the Book of the Gospels to the credence table or to another appropriate and dignified place.

—GIRM, 175

See also GIRM, 134.

Background

At the conclusion of the Gospel, the deacon or priest finishes with a formula, and the people make a response.[1] Then he kisses the book and recites another formula quietly, this one for the forgiveness of sins.

"Praise to you, Christ," existed in the 1570 Missal, but new to the current rite is making it part of a dialogue between the ordained minister and the people. While revising the Order of Mass, Study Group 10 at first permitted an acclamation after the Gospel, but did not specify a particular text for it until later.[2]

That text, "Praise to you, Lord Jesus Christ," affirms the people's belief in the presence of Jesus Christ in his proclaimed word. The same is true of their text before the Gospel, "Glory to you, O Lord," and in the acclamations that

---

1   The revised English translation says, "All reply," but they are not replying to the priest or deacon. They respond with an acclamation to Christ.

2   Barba, p. 377, 440.

substitute for the Alleluia during the season of Lent. "When the Sacred Scriptures are read in the Church, God himself speaks to his people, and Christ, present in his own word, proclaims the Gospel."[3]

Following the proclamation of the Gospel in *Ordo Romanus I*,[4] the book was held by a sub-deacon so that several ministers could kiss it.

In *Ordo Romanus V*, probably compiled in the late ninth century, the subdeacon held it while all the ministers and all the people kissed it.[5]

The private prayer of the priest or deacon at the end appeared already in the 1570 Missal and remains unchanged.

---

3   GIRM, 29.
4   OR I:64.

5   OR V:38.

Questions for Discussion and Reflection

1. How do the people acknowledge the presence of Jesus Christ in the proclaimed Gospel?

_____

_____

_____

2. There is no rubric calling for the priest or deacon to raise the *Book of the Gospels* when announcing the conclusion of the proclamation. Why would this be?

_____

_____

_____

3. When the priest or deacon announces, "The Gospel of the Lord," does he wait for the response before kissing the book? Why or why not?

_____

_____

_____

Does the priest or deacon say the concluding formula in a low voice? Why is that important?

_____

_____

_____

HOMILY

17.   Then follows the Homily, which is to be preached by a Priest or Deacon on all Sundays and Holydays of Obligation; on other days, it is recommended.

> The Homily is part of the Liturgy and is highly recommended, for it is necessary for the nurturing of the Christian life. It should be an explanation of some aspect of the readings from Sacred Scripture or of another text from the Ordinary or the Proper of the Mass of the day and should take into account both the mystery being celebrated and the particular needs of the listeners.
>
> —GIRM, 65
>
> See also GIRM, 45, 56, 66, 136, and 171c.

Background

In practice the homily usually springs from the scriptures of the day to exhort the faithful to a better way of life. However, it may fittingly reflect on texts from the Order of Mass or the prayers and chants of the day.

The homily has antecedents in passages from the New Testament. On the road to Emmaus, Jesus explained the scriptures to two disciples before breaking bread with them.[1] Paul held a discussion with the faithful in Troas when he met with them to break bread.[2]

In the second century, Justin the Martyr describes a Liturgy of the Word. "When the reader has finished, he who presides over those gathered admonishes and challenges them to imitate these beautiful things."[3] Many of the Church Fathers are remembered for their sermons. But no homily is mentioned in *Ordo Romanus I*, which may indicate that it had fallen into disuse by the eighth century.[4] In time, preachers spoke about moral and doctrinal issues from the pulpit, which were valuable, but the homily had lost its integration with the liturgy and its texts.[5]

The Second Vatican Council reset the purpose of the homily in its *Constitution on the Sacred Liturgy*.

> By means of the homily, the mysteries of the faith and the guiding principles of the christian life are expounded from the sacred text during the course of the liturgical year. The homily is strongly recommended since it forms part of the liturgy itself. In fact, at those Masses which are celebrated on Sundays and holydays of obligation, with the people assisting, it should not be omitted except for a serious reason.[6]

A short time later, Pope Paul VI put some of the prescriptions of the Constitution into effect in his 1964 *Motu Proprio Sacram Liturgiam*. There he said, "On the date already established, the norms of art. 52 shall take effect, namely, that there be a Homily during Mass on Sundays and holydays of obligation."[7]

Homilies vary in quality from preacher to preacher and from Sunday to Sunday. But overall the faithful have a better opportunity for enrichment on the scriptural and liturgical texts of the Mass than they did before the Council.

If catechumens are present, they may be dismissed after the homily.

---

1   See Luke 24:27.

2   See Acts 20:7–12. In a tragicomic moment, one of the listeners, Eutychus, sank into a deep sleep because of the length of Paul's talk, and fell out the window. Paul revived him.

3   *Apology* 1:67. Cited in CCC, 1345.

4   Cabié, *History of the Mass*, p. 51.

5   Cabié, *The Church at Prayer*, 2:154.

6   CSL, 52.

7   DOL, 281.

Questions for Discussion and Reflection

1. Who delivers the homily in your worshipping community?

_____

_____

2. How often is a homily preached?

_____

_____

3. What texts form the basis for the homily?

_____

_____

4. What are the strengths and weaknesses of the homilies you hear?

_____

_____

_____

PROFESSION OF FAITH

18.   At the end of the Homily, the Symbol or Profession of Faith or Creed, when prescribed, is either sung or said:

I believe in one God,
the Father almighty,
maker of heaven and earth,
of all things visible and invisible.

I believe in one Lord Jesus Christ,
the Only Begotten Son of God,
born of the Father before all ages.
God from God, Light from Light,
true God from true God,
begotten, not made, consubstantial with the Father;
through him all things were made.
For us men and for our salvation
he came down from heaven,

The Creed is to be sung or said by the Priest together with the people on Sundays and Solemnities. It may be said also at particular celebrations of a more solemn character.

If it is sung, it is intoned by the Priest or, if appropriate, by a cantor or by the choir. It is then sung either by everybody together or by the people alternating with the choir.

If it is not sung, it is to be recited by everybody together or by two choirs responding one to the other.

—GIRM, 68

See also GIRM, 41, 43, 67, 137, 275b, and 309.

and by the Holy Spirit was incarnate of the Virgin Mary,
and became man.

For our sake he was crucified under Pontius Pilate,
he suffered death and was buried,
and rose again on the third day
in accordance with the Scriptures.
He ascended into heaven
and is seated at the right hand of the Father.
He will come again in glory
to judge the living and the dead
and his kingdom will have no end.

I believe in the Holy Spirit, the Lord, the giver of life,
who proceeds from the Father and the Son,
who with the Father and the Son is adored and glorified,
who has spoken through the prophets.

I believe in one, holy, catholic and apostolic Church.
I confess one Baptism for the forgiveness of sins
and I look forward to the resurrection of the dead
and the life of the world to come. Amen.

Background

The Creed unifies the voices of the assembly into the common faith it professes. It is the first statement following the dismissal of catechumens, who are still preparing to profess their faith on the day of their Baptism.

After the death of Jesus, it took the Church several centuries to formulate the Creed it now professes. In the middle of the second century, a catechetical device for teaching the faith appears in the *Epistula Apostolorum* (*Letter of the Apostles*). It interprets the five loaves that Jesus used in the miracle as an allegory for faith:

> They are a picture of our faith concerning the great Christianity; and that is in the Father, the ruler of the entire world, and in Jesus Christ our Savior, and in the Holy Spirit, the Paraclete, and in the Holy Church, and in the forgiveness of sins.[1]

A century or so later, the *Apostolic Tradition* describes the initiation practices of the early Church. There, those to be baptized are asked to profess their belief in the Trinity in question and answer form.[2]

From this practice grew the desire for a Creed articulating the faith of the Church. Its rudimentary form has been handed down as the Apostles' Creed. The need became more critical in the fourth century, when heretical movements tore at the fabric of the Church, and people sought clarity for their faith. The Councils of Nicaea (325) and Constantinople (381) took up the task and burnished the version now known

---

1 Cited in Luke Timothy Johnson, *The Creed: What Christians Believe and Why It Matters* (New York, New York: Doubleday, 2003), p. 23.
2 AT 21:12-18.

as the Niceno-Constantinopolitan Creed, or simply the Nicene Creed. In 589 the Council of Toledo added the Latin word *filioque* to express the Western Church's belief that the Holy Spirit proceeds not only from the Father but also from the Son. This has remained a highly disputed point with Eastern Rite Churches that have never accepted the additional word.

The same Council of Toledo required all churches in its region to profess the Creed together before the Lord's Prayer on Sundays.[3] The practice had probably begun already in the East.[4] Still, it took time for the practice to reach Rome. The Creed is not mentioned in *Ordo Romanus I,* but it does appear in *Ordo Romanus V.*[5] Abbot Bernard of Reichenau accompanied Emperor Henry II to Rome in 1014 and was sur-

prised that the Creed was not recited at Mass.[6] According to the same source, Rome thought that reciting the Creed was unnecessary there because the city had remained in solidarity with Saint Peter, and hence had not been infected by any heresy. Upon further discussion, Rome adopted the German custom.

With the 1570 Missal it became the custom to genuflect each week at the words of the Incarnation. The 1970 Missal changed this to a profound bow made in the direction of the altar. The genuflection was retained only for Masses on the solemnities of the Annunciation (March 25) and Nativity of the Lord (Christmas).

Congregations often recite the Creed without intense thought, but week by week, generation after generation, these words unite the faith of the Church around the world and across the ages. It gives a weekly assent to the core of Christian belief.

---

3 Canon 2. *Sacrorum conciliorum nova et amplissima collectio,* Ed. Johannes Dominicus Mansi et al. Florence: Antonius Zatta Venetus, 9:991.

4 Cabié, *The Church at Prayer* 2:131.

5 OR V:40.

6 Bernonis, *Libellus de quibusdam rebus ad missae officium pertinentibus* 2, PL 142:1060–1061.

Questions for Discussion and Reflection

1. How well is the Creed professed in your community?

_____

_____

_____

2. Is the Creed part of the weekly gathering every Sunday? Why is this important?

_____

_____

_____

3. Who begins the Creed? How? And why?

_____

_____

_____

4. Do you ever sing the Creed? Is it sung in unison or in alteration?

_____

_____

_____

5. How is the Creed made known to catechumens? To Confirmation candidates? To parents of children to be baptized?

_____

_____

_____

6. The rubrics call for all to make a profound bow toward the altar during the words of the Incarnation. Why is this important? Is it happening in your church?

_____

_____

_____

7. Do you genuflect during the Creed on March 25 (Annunciation of the Lord) and December 25 (Nativity of the Lord)?

_____

_____

_____

8. The Creed is not listed among the proper uses of the ambo. Where is the priest standing for the Creed?

_____

_____

_____

See also *Directory for Masses with Children,* 39 and 49.

19.   Instead of the Niceno-Constantinopolitan Creed, especially during Lent and Easter Time, the baptismal Symbol of the Roman Church, known as the Apostles' Creed, may be used.

I believe in God,
the Father almighty,
Creator of heaven and earth,
and in Jesus Christ, his only Son, our Lord,

At the words that follow, up to and including **the Virgin Mary,** all bow.

who was conceived by the Holy Spirit,
born of the Virgin Mary,
suffered under Pontius Pilate,
was crucified, died and was buried;
he descended into hell;
on the third day he rose again from the dead;

he ascended into heaven,
and is seated at the right hand of God the Father almighty;
from there he will come to judge the living and the dead.

I believe in the Holy Spirit,
the holy catholic Church,
the communion of saints,
the forgiveness of sins,
the resurrection of the body,
and life everlasting. Amen.

Background

The current rite provides two options: the Nicene Creed and the Apostles' Creed. The latter had ecumenical advantages because of the *filioque* in the former. In preparing the new Order of Mass, it was proposed even to replace the Nicene Creed with the Apostles' Creed, or at least to provide it as an alternative for the sake of children or those unschooled in the faith.[1]

In the end, the Order of Mass was originally published in Latin and in English only with the Nicene Creed. However, in 1973 the *Directory for Masses with Children* permitted the use of the Apostles' Creed,[2] and in 1985 it appeared in the revised Order of Mass together with the Nicene Creed for this reason. In the United States of America, the Nicene Creed has been used almost exclusively on Sundays; whereas in Canada an indult was obtained for the use of the Apostles' Creed, which has been the text in force every Sunday at a typical parish Mass.

Now both Creeds appear in the Missal, and for yet another reason. The Apostles' Creed is offered not for its ecumenical appeal, and not for ease of comprehension with children, but because it is "the baptismal Symbol of the Roman Church," making it especially fitting for the seasons of Lent and Easter. Easter is the ideal day and season for celebrating Baptism because

Both the Apostles' Creed and the Nicene Creed appear in the Missal.

Baptism participates in the Resurrection of Christ. The Apostles' Creed has direct links to the baptismal promises. The presentation of the Creed and the return of the Creed from the *Rite of Christian Initiation of Adults* favor the use of the Apostles' Creed, which appears as the first option.

---

1   Barba, p. 360.
2   DMC, 49.

Questions for Discussion and Reflection

1. On what occasions does your community use the Apostles' Creed?

_____

_____

_____

2. Do people experience both the Apostles' Creed and the Nicene Creed?

_____

_____

_____

3. In popular piety, which Creed begins the recitation of the Rosary?

_____

_____

_____

PRAYER OF THE FAITHFUL

20.　Then follows the Universal Prayer, that is, the Prayer of the Faithful or Bidding Prayers.

In the Universal Prayer or Prayer of the Faithful, the people respond in some sense to the Word of God which they have received in faith and, exercising the office of their baptismal Priesthood, offer prayers to God for the salvation of all. It is desirable that there usually be such a form of prayer in Masses celebrated with the people, so that petitions may be offered for holy Church, for those who govern with authority over us, for those weighed down by various needs, for all humanity, and for the salvation of the whole world.

The series of intentions is usually to be:
a) for the needs of the Church;
b) for public authorities and the salvation of the whole world;
c) for those burdened by any kind of difficulty;
d) for the local community. . . .

—GIRM, 69–70

See also GIRM, 40, 43, 71, 138, 139, 171d, 177, and 197.

Background

All the faithful make their petitions known to God. In doing so, they exercise their baptismal ministry as the priestly people.

The Order of Mass gives three different names for this part because it is variously titled in different parts of the world: the Universal Prayer, the Prayer of the Faithful, or Bidding Prayers. It is universal because the community prays for the needs of all the world, not just local ones. It is the prayer "of the faithful" because catechumens have been dismissed, and the faithful are exercising their priestly ministry. They are "bidding" because they take the form of a litany, and the one announcing the intentions bids the people to pray for them.

The practice of praying for specific groups is recommended in the First Letter to Timothy, though the context makes no mention of the Eucharist.[1] However in the second century, Justin the Martyr says that such petitions followed the readings from scripture. "Then we all rise together and offer prayers for ourselves . . . and for all others, wherever they may be, so that we may be found righteous by our life and actions, and faithful to the commandments, so as to obtain eternal salvation."[2] A detailed example can be found in the fourth century *Apostolic Constitutions*,[3] where a long list of petitions is preserved.

1　See 1 Timothy 2:1–4.
2　*Apology* 1:67. Cited in CCC, 1345.
3　AC 8:10–11.

Some early manuscripts credit the fifth century Pope Gelasius as the source of this litany in the liturgy. After petitions, people responded, "Lord, hear and have mercy," or "Kyrie, eleison."[4] Once the Kyrie had taken its place at the start of the Eucharist, the prayers of intercession began to disappear.[5]

A parallel practice developed in the tenth century, during a service that included prayers for various needs, instruction, announcements, and promulgation of commands. Because French churches performing the practice had a grill that separated the sanctuary and the nave, and upon which notices were posted, the service was named for the grill, "Prône" in French.[6] According to Regino of Prüm (+915) these were adopted into the liturgy, on feast days and Sundays after the sermon.[7]

The 1570 Missal shows only a trace of these prayers. Before the Offertory begins, the celebrant says, "Let us pray," but no prayers follow.

It may be all that was left of the practice that began in the early Church and resurfaced in a different form in the Middle Ages. Study Group 10, aware of this history, recommended restoring the Prayer of the Faithful.[8]

Today the Prayer of the Faithful is integral to every celebration of the Mass. It is the most freely composed part of the entire liturgy, except for the Homily. There are guidelines for its content, but its design expects the local community

> Today the Prayer of the Faithful is integral to every celebration of the Mass. It is the most freely composed part of the entire liturgy, except for the Homily.

to formulate the petitions for which it will pray. Assigning the listing of the petitions to the deacon harkens back to the practice in the fourth century *Apostolic Constitutions*. It also underscores his role as the one responsible for charity in the community, the one who would be most aware of local needs. Still, another minister may read the petitions. Because they are part of the Liturgy of the Word and grow out from the scriptures, the petitions may be led from the ambo.

---

4   Cabié, *The Church at Prayer* 2:72.

5   Cabié, *The Church at Prayer* 2:73.

6   "Prône," *The New Catholic Encyclopedia, Second Edition.*

7   *De ecclesiasticis disciplinis et religione christiana collectus* 190, PL 132:224.

---

8   Barba, pp. 392, 418, and 441.

Questions for Discussion and Reflection

1. In your community, who writes the Prayer of the Faithful? Do you script the introduction, the petitions, the response, and the closing prayer? Or only the petitions?

_____

_____

_____

2. Who reads the petitions? Why?

_____

_____

_____

3. From where are the petitions led? Why?

_____

_____

_____

4. How do you incorporate the contemporary needs of society into the prayer of your local Church?

_____

_____

_____

THE LITURGY OF
THE EUCHARIST

PREPARATION OF THE GIFTS

21. When all this has been done, the Offertory Chant begins. Meanwhile, the ministers place the corporal, the purificator, the chalice, the pall, and the Missal on the altar.

> . . . First of all, the altar or Lord's table, which is the center of the whole Liturgy of the Eucharist, is made ready when on it are placed the corporal, purificator, Missal and chalice (unless this last is prepared at the credence table). . . .
>
> —GIRM, 73
>
> See also GIRM, 37b, 74, 118c, 139, 142, 178, 190, 306, and 313.

Background

The Liturgy of the Eucharist has two high points: the Eucharistic Prayer and the sharing of Holy Communion. The other elements prepare for and flow from these key moments. In the Eucharistic Prayer the community prays that the Holy Spirit will change the bread and

> The set of ceremonies that precedes the Eucharistic Prayer is called the Preparation of the Gifts. The altar is prepared, the gifts are brought forward, and God is praised for them.

wine into the Body and Blood of Christ. During Holy Communion the faithful share in the sacrament, establishing their union with Christ and with one another.

The set of ceremonies that precedes the Eucharistic Prayer is called the Preparation of the Gifts.[1] The altar is prepared, the gifts are brought forward, and God is praised for them.

The Offertory Chant probably existed as early as the fifth century in some form. Augustine defends the practice against a certain Hilary, who was opposed to singing Psalms "before the offering."[2] As the procession became more elaborate in the Middle Ages, so did the singing.[3] In the 1570 Missal, the priest read the offertory antiphon immediately after saying, "Let us pray." Texts for the antiphon are proper to the days and seasons of the liturgical year, and a book called the *Liber usualis* offered musical settings for all the parts of the Mass, including the Offertory Chant.

In preparing the 1970 Missal, Study Group 10 considered restoring verses to the Offertory

Chant, which had been lost over the course of time.[4] But the reform valued the participation of the people and the simplification of the rites, so the texts for the Offertory Chant were eventually removed from the Missal, though they can be found in the collection of chants for mass called the *Graduale Romanum*, and the simplified version called the *Graduale Simplex*. The Missal itself contains the text for only one Offertory Chant, at the Evening Mass of the Lord's Supper on Holy Thursday. The second edition of the Missal said that the chant was omitted if it were not sung,[5] but now it says that singing may always accompany the Preparation of the Gifts, even if there is no procession.[6]

The preparation of the altar was a practical matter that evolved into a detailed ritual involving the elements to be placed there. In *Ordo Romanus I*, the deacon goes to the altar as the acolyte brings forward the chalice and corporal.[7] The complexity of the ritual was diminished with the 1570 Missal because the entire Mass was celebrated at the altar. The vessels and cloths were there from the beginning; a priest typically carried the chalice, paten and host with him in the entrance procession, and set them on the altar at the beginning of the Mass.

In the current rite, the Order of Mass expects that the altar has been bare up to this point, except perhaps for the candles, and for the Book of the Gospels, which has since been carried to the ambo. Ministers—not the priest—bring various elements to the altar. The corporal

---

1   See GIRM, 73, heading.
2   *Retractiones* 2:11. CCL, 57:98.
3   Jungmann 2:26–27.

4   Barba, p. 262.
5   See GIRM, 50.
6   See GIRM, 74.
7   OR I:67.

is to be laid there at this time, though many worshipping communities keep it on the altar from one Mass to the next. The purificator, which will be used to wipe the rim of the chalice, may also be carried to the altar. The paten is not mentioned because the bread will be sitting on it when it is brought forward. The pall—the stiff square that may cover the chalice—is optional, and is mentioned only here in the Missal. The priest is never told what to do with it once it appears on the altar. The Missal is also brought forward at this time. If the priest uses a bookstand, it would logically come as well. In most churches the Missal is set to the side and turned toward the priest, a placement that was necessary for the 1570 Missal because the altar was so narrow; however, turning the book is not specified in the 1970 Missal.

Questions for Discussion and Reflection

1. Does your community sing a chant, song, or hymn during the Preparation of the Gifts? How do you decide which one? If you do not sing, how do you decide that?

_____

_____

_____

2. Who sets the altar? Which ministers take part? How much of the altar is set before Mass begins? Why is it important to have a bare altar at the beginning of Mass?

_____

_____

_____

3. Does the paten come to the altar separate from the chalice?

_____

_____

_____

5. If you serve Holy Communion under both forms, how do all the chalices come to the altar? Do the purificators come forward at this time as well?

_____

_____

_____

6. How many corporals do you use? Is one sufficient for the needs of the vessels that will be set on the altar?

_____

_____

_____

7. Where does your priest like to have the Missal sit on the altar? Why?

_____

_____

_____

22. It is desirable that the faithful express their participation by making an offering, bringing forward bread and wine for the celebration of the Eucharist and perhaps other gifts to relieve the needs of the Church and of the poor.

It is desirable that the participation of the faithful be expressed by an offering, whether of bread and wine for the celebration of the Eucharist or of other gifts to relieve the needs of the Church and of the poor.

The offerings of the faithful are received by the Priest, assisted by the acolyte or other minister. The bread and wine for the Eucharist are carried to the Celebrant, who places them on the altar, while other gifts are put in another suitable place (cf. no. 73).

—GIRM, 140

If Communion from the chalice is done by drinking directly from the chalice, a chalice of a sufficiently large size or several chalices are prepared. However, care should be taken lest beyond what is needed of the Blood of Christ remains to be consumed at the end of the celebration.

—GIRM, 285a

By reason of the sign, it is required that the material for the Eucharistic celebration truly have the appearance of food. . . .

—GIRM, 321

See also GIRM, 72.3, 73, 83, 85, 105c, 118c, 282, 320, 322, and 323.

Background

Once the altar is prepared, the bread, wine, and gifts for the needs of the Church and the poor are brought forward. In most parishes, ushers take up a collection first, so that these offerings can be carried together.

Such an offering is apparent all the way back to the second century in the community of Justin the Martyr.

> Then someone brings bread and a cup of water and wine mixed together to him who presides over the brethren.[1]
>
> They who have the means and who are willing, give freely what they wish, according to each one's preference; and what is collected is placed in reserve with the president, who provides help to the orphans, widows, and those who, through sickness or any other cause, are in need, and prisoners, and traveling strangers; in a word, he takes care of all who are in need.[2]

Deacons hand the offerings to the Bishop at the Eucharist in the *Apostolic Tradition*.[3] They do the same in the fourth-century *Apostolic Constitutions*. "Let the deacons bring the gifts to the bishop at the altar; and let the presbyters stand on his right hand, and on his left, as disciples stand before their Master."[4]

Cyprian encouraged the third-century faithful to bring their own offerings to the church.[5] According to Jerome, when people came for the Eucharist in the fourth century,

---

1 Justin, *First Apology* 67. Cited in CCC, 1345.

2 Justin, *First Apology* 67. SChr 507:310–311; translation PT.

3 AT 4:2.

4 AC 8:12, 3; translation PT.

5 *De opere et eleemosynis* 15 CCL 3a:64–65.

they brought their gifts as well as their intentions.[6] The Council of Elvira (c. 305) discouraged Bishops from accepting an offering from someone who did not participate at the Eucharist.[7] By the twelfth-century Honorius of Autun tells of people bringing money instead of bread.[8]

The 1570 Missal made no provision for the faithful to bring forward the bread and wine during the Eucharist. The collection was taken up, but ushers usually put it away.

Study Group 10 knew that these preparatory rites needed much work. They wished to restore the procession of the gifts, even though the faithful no longer brought their own bread and wine from home.[9] Pope Paul VI had questions about the development of these rites,[10] and he would have known the custom of the Ambrosian Rite, which had representatives of the people bringing up the gifts.[11] The study group valued this kind of participation as an exercise of the priestly ministry of the faithful.[12] The procession of gifts was implemented in the 1970 Missal, and it has become common at a parish Sunday Mass.

6   *In Hieremiam Prophetam* 2:108, CCL 74:116; *In Hiezechielem Prophetam* 6:18, CCL 75:238.

7   Canon 28, *Conciliengeschichte*, ed. Carl Joseph von Hefele (Freiburg im Breisgau: Herder'sche Verlagshandlung, 1873) I:167.

8   *Gemma animae* I:66, PL 172:564–565.

9   Barba, p. 419.

10   Barba, p. 188.

11   Barba, p. 254.

12   Barba, p. 261.

Questions for Discussion and Reflection

1. In your community, what elements are brought forward in the procession of the gifts? Why?

_____

_____

_____

2. Is the priest's bread on a paten separate from everyone else's bread? Why?

_____

_____

_____

3. Do you prepare sufficient wine for all to receive under both species? Why?

_____

_____

_____

4. Who brings the gifts forward? How are they determined?

_____

_____

_____

5. How is the collection taken up? Do a variety of ministers assist?

_____

_____

_____

6. For what purposes does your community take up a second collection? When does it take place at Mass? Why then?

_____

_____

_____

7. Are there occasions when you take up some other offering for the poor? How is that best done?

_____

_____

_____

8. Where does the priest stand to receive the gifts? Why there?

_____

_____

_____

_____

23. The Priest, standing at the altar, takes the paten with the bread and holds it slightly raised above the altar with both hands, saying in a low voice:

Blessed are you, Lord God of all creation,
for through your goodness we have received
the bread we offer you:
fruit of the earth and work of human hands,
it will become for us the bread of life.

Then he places the paten with the bread on the corporal.

If, however, the Offertory Chant is not sung, the Priest may speak these words aloud; at the end, the people may acclaim:

Blessed be God for ever.

. . . The offerings of the faithful are received by the Priest, assisted by the acolyte or other minister. The bread and wine for the Eucharist are carried to the Celebrant, who places them on the altar, while other gifts are put in another suitable place (cf. no. 73).

—GIRM, 140

. . . If, however, there is no Offertory Chant and the organ is not played, in the presentation of the bread and wine the Priest may say the formulas of blessing aloud and the people acclaim, *Blessed be God for ever.*

—GIRM, 142

See also GIRM, 73, 74, 75, 100, 141, 178, 190, and 306.

Background

The priest receives the bread and wine at an appropriate place. He says a prayer blessing God for the bread, and then he sets it on the altar. All these steps are significant in this sequence. The accompanying prayers are said aloud if the assembly is not singing an Offertory Chant. If they do sing, the prayers may be said quietly, and the acclamation, "Blessed be God for ever" is omitted.

With the addition of the procession of the gifts to the Mass, the reception of the gifts gained importance. Prior to the 1970 Missal, the bread was already on the altar when the priest began Mass, and a server brought him the cruet of wine. Now the procession represents that the gifts come from the people, and the priest receives them.

Before he places them on the altar, the priest praises God. The people may make an acclamation in response. Study Group 10 wanted the people to have some verbal participation in the

Preparation of the Gifts, which they did not have before. The dialogue upon taking the bread is optional; the priest may say it quietly, but only if the people are busy singing something. The voice of the people is intended to be heard in some way during the Preparation of the Gifts.[1]

The generation that has used these prayers may be unaware how new they are. Prior to the 1970 Missal, the priest recited a completely different set. Study Group 10 found these prayers deficient for several reasons. The first asked God to receive "this spotless host," an expression that would have made more sense after the consecration. There followed a prayer that said, "We offer to you, O Lord, the chalice of salvation," but the offering belonged after the consecration, and the chalice would more properly be called "of salvation" at that same time. The plural form, "We offer," came from the Mozarabic tradition, and may have indicated that the deacon held the cup as the priest recited the text.[2] Another prayer invoked the Holy Spirit to bless this sacrifice, but an epiclesis belonged in the Eucharistic Prayer, not in the Preparation of the Gifts. There was also a prayer addressed to the Trinity, which broke from the Roman tradition of addressing prayer to the Father, through the Son and in the Holy Spirit. Putting all this under the heading of "offertory" only added to the confusion; the real offering of the sacrifice takes place during the Eucharistic Prayer.

As with other private prayers of the priest, these were added to the Mass over a period of centuries and were not part of the earliest strata of Eucharistic worship. Hence, the study group felt freer to adjust these texts. However, having researched the tradition, it was difficult for them to find substitute texts that did not anticipate the Eucharistic Prayer.[3] Various options were proposed before settling on the ones that appear in the revised Missal today. That formula, with its acclamation, "Blessed be God for ever," was influenced by the second-century *Didache*.[4]

At one point the Latin verb was changed from *fiat* to *fiet*—that is, from "may it become" to "it will become," in order to avoid any perception that elements of the preparation of the gifts were consecratory.[5]

The new text emphasizes the generosity of God, the produce of the earth, human labor, and the Eucharist for which these gifts are brought. When it was first proposed, it did not include the words "we offer" because the text was intended to eliminate any anticipation of sacrifice, offering, or epiclesis.[6]

Given this context, it is surprising that the words "we offer" were added. They existed in the 1570 Missal only at the words pertaining to the chalice. Pope Paul VI himself decided to include the verb *offerimus* in the new texts—both the one for the bread and for the wine, perhaps to appease some theologians who wanted to retain something of the previous offertory.[7] So the texts still say "we offer," but the meaning has more to do with the bread on hand than the body of Christ that it will become: the present offering of the people, rather than the offering of Christ soon to be entered.[8]

---

1 Barba, p. 274.
2 *Missale mixtum secundum regulam b. Isidori dictum Mozarabes*, PL 85:536; translation PT.

3 Barba, p. 419.
4 Barba, p. 272.
5 Ibid.
6 Barba, p. 674.
7 Bugnini, p. 371.
8 Oury, p. 90.

Questions for Discussion and Reflection

1. How clear is it that the bread goes from the procession, into the hands of the priest, where it is held— not lifted—for words of praise, and then set upon the corporal?

_____

_____

_____

2. How often does your community speak the acclamation? How often do they sing? Do they do both? Do they ever do neither? Why? Does the music customarily end when the priest receives the gifts or after the washing of the hands? Why?

_____

_____

_____

3. How does your community understand the meaning of the word "offertory"? Does it mean the offering of Jesus? Their own offering of bread and wine? The collection? The music? How clear is it that the offering of the sacrifice of the Mass takes place later?

_____

_____

_____

24.   The Deacon, or the Priest, pours wine and a little water into the chalice, saying quietly:

By the mystery of this water and wine
may we come to share in the divinity of Christ
who humbled himself to share in our humanity.

After this, as the minister presents the cruets, the Priest stands at the side of the altar and pours wine and a little water into the chalice, saying quietly, *Per huius aquae* (*By the mystery of this water*). . . .

—GIRM, 142

See also GIRM, 33 and 178; *Redemptionis Sacramentum* (RS), 106.

Backgound

Water is added to the wine, a ceremony of much antiquity. A text about the Incarnation accompanies this action, which is designed to take place at the side of the altar, or even at the credence table. A deacon performs this action, or, in his absence, the priest.

This preparation appeared in some of the earliest records of the Eucharist. Justin the Martyr records this second-century practice: "Then someone brings bread and a cup of water and wine mixed together to him who presides over the brethren."[1] Cyprian interprets the practice in one of his letters from the third century:

Thus in the sanctifying cup of the Lord, water alone cannot be offered, as wine alone cannot be. For if a person offers wine only, it starts to become the blood of Christ without us. But if the water is alone, it starts

to become the people without Christ. But when both are mingled, and are joined with one another by a close union, a spiritual and heavenly sacrament is completed.[2]

The practice probably originated at a time when the wine, in general, was thicker and needed to be thinned before drinking.

Ordo Romanus I instructs the subdeacon to obtain water from the schola and hand it to the archdeacon, who poured it into the prepared chalice in the form of a cross.[3] The 1474 Missal included a prayer to accompany the mixture, which endured through the life of the 1570 Missal and was abbreviated for the 1970 Missal. It was inspired by the Collect for Christmas Day, probably composed by Leo the Great.[4]

The first drafts of the revised Mass eliminated this prayer altogether, probably because it was too allegorical—applying the Christmas

---

1   Justin, *First Apology 67*. Cited in CCC, 1345.

2   *Epistvla* 63:2-3, CCL 3C:407–408; translation PT.
3   OR I:80.
4   *Veronese* 1239.

mystery to the mixture of the wine and water.[5] But some wanted to have the priest say it aloud so that all could appreciate its content.[6] In the end it remained in the Mass as a private prayer in an abbreviated form.

If more than one cup is to be used, all of them are prepared at this time. "[T]he pouring of the Blood of Christ after the consecration from one vessel to another is completely to be avoided, lest anything should happen that would be to the detriment of so great a mystery."[7]

5 Barba, p. 611.
6 Barba, p. 674.

7 RS, 106.

Questions for Discussion and Reflection

1. Who adds the water to the wine, the deacon or the priest? Where does this take place? Why?

_____

_____

_____

2. Is the prayer offered in a quiet voice? Where has the chalice been prior to this time? Why has it been there?

_____

_____

_____

3. The Order of Mass presumes that only one vessel is holding wine at this point. If you use multiple cups, does the priest or deacon pour water into all of them? Why or why not?

_____

_____

_____

25. The Priest then takes the chalice and holds it slightly raised above the altar with both hands, saying in a low voice:

Blessed are you, Lord God of all creation,
for through your goodness we have received
the wine we offer you:
fruit of the vine and work of human hands,
it will become our spiritual drink.

Then he places the chalice on the corporal.

If, however, the Offertory Chant is not sung, the Priest may speak these words aloud; at the end, the people may acclaim:

Blessed be God for ever.

. . . He returns to the middle of the altar and with both hands raises the chalice a little, and says quietly, *Benedíctus es, Domine* (*Blessed are you, Lord God*). Then he places the chalice on the corporal and, if appropriate, covers it with a pall. . . .

—GIRM, 142

See also GIRM, 74 and 178.

Background

Once the chalice has been prepared, the priest praises God for the wine, the people may make their response, and then he sets the chalice on the corporal.

The appearance of a separate text for the chalice dates only to the fourteenth century. Prior to this time the priest said prayers over the bread and the wine together, as had been done in the Dominican and Carthusian liturgies.[1] The text in the 1570 Missal, which mentioned the offering of the saving chalice, endured for several centuries. Study Group 10 tried several other texts to replace it, notably one that quoted Proverbs 9:1–2: "Wisdom has built herself a house, has mixed the wine and set the table. Glory to you, O God, for ever."[2] A slightly more elaborate version was already in place as the first antiphon for lauds on the feast of Corpus Christi, which later became the solemnity of the Most Holy Body and Blood of Christ.[3] In the end, though, this was changed to the text currently in use.

---

1 Oury, p. 83.

2 Barba, p. 266.
3 Barba, p. 420.

Questions for Discussion and Reflection

1. On what occasions does the priest say this text aloud?

_____

_____

_____

2. Does it ever make sense to say this second text aloud, having recited the first one quietly?

_____

_____

_____

3. If the people have been singing at the Preparation of the Gifts, when does the music end? Why?

_____

_____

_____

26. After this, the Priest, bowing profoundly, says quietly:

See GIRM, 33, 143, and 275b.

With humble spirit and contrite heart
may we be accepted by you, O Lord,
and may our sacrifice in your sight this day
be pleasing to you, Lord God.

Background

The priest offers a private prayer, humbly asking God to accept the people and the sacrifice that will be offered.

The prayer originates from the story of the three young men in the fiery furnace.[1] Azariah offers this prayer from within the flames, asking that the sacrifice of his very life be pleasing to God. The priest, mindful of his sins, offers his suffering together with the gifts on the altar.

This is a private prayer, not to be said aloud. It was already in place for the 1474 Missal and has endured all the way through the current rite. In fact, Study Group 10 never proposed a change to this text. It seemed an appropriate prayer for the circumstances.

---

1   See Daniel 3:39.

Questions for Discussion and Reflection

1. The priest is to make this prayer in a low voice. Does he? Why is this important?

_____

_____

_____

2. The priest is to make a profound bow while saying this prayer. Does he? Why is that important?

_____

_____

_____

27.   If appropriate, he also incenses the offerings, the cross, and the altar. A Deacon or other minister then incenses the Priest and the people.

. . . The altar is incensed with single swings of the thurible in this way:

a) if the altar is freestanding with respect to the wall, the Priest incenses walking around it;

b) if the altar is not freestanding, the Priest incenses it while walking first to the right hand side, then to the left.

The cross, if situated on the altar or near it, is incensed by the Priest before he incenses the altar; otherwise, he incenses it when he passes in front of it.

The Priest incenses the offerings with three swings of the thurible or by making the Sign of the Cross over the offerings with the thurible before going on to incense the cross and the altar.

—GIRM, 277

See also GIRM, 75, 144, 178, 190, and 276d.

Background

Incense usually signifies a solemn occasion, the holiness of that which is incensed, and the prayers of the people lifting toward God. During the Preparation of the Gifts, the offerings, the altar, the cross, the priest, and the people all may be incensed.

The practice arrived fairly late in the history of the Mass, and it did not originate in Rome. Incense was being used quite elaborately in Gaul, more sparingly in Rome by comparison. But the Gallic observance spread. Amalarius of Metz (+850) knew the custom of incensing the gifts.[1] The eleventh-century *Pontifical of Sées* called for incensing the offerings, the altar and the ministers, together with the prayers that appeared later in the 1570 Missal.[2] Solemn ceremonies called for the priest to incense the offerings three times in the form of a cross and three times in the form of a circle.[3] These were greatly simplified for the 1970 Missal.

Study Group 10 considered moving the incensing of the priest and the people to the beginning of the Mass, and incensing only the gifts at this time.[4] The longstanding custom has remained, however, and it indicates that the bread, the wine, the priest, and the people will all be part of the offering from the altar. The two incense prayers from the 1570 Missal were eliminated. The priest blesses the incense without any words, making the Sign of the Cross with his hand.

1   *De ecclesiasticis officiis libri iv* 3:19, PL 105:1130D.
2   *Ex Codice Tiliano*, PL 78:249.
3   Innocentius Wapelhorst, *Compendium Sacrae Liturgiae juxta Ritum Romanum* (New York: Benziger Brothers, 1925), p. 172.
4   Barba, p. 249.

Questions for Discussion and Reflection

1. On what occasions do you use incense for the Preparation of the Gifts?

_____

_____

_____

2. How well does the priest observe the more limited instructions for incensing and bowing?

_____

_____

_____

3. Who incenses the priest and the people? Is this done very often? Why? How does the incensing of the people take place?

_____

_____

_____

4. The rubrics are silent about the posture of the people. Do they stand for the incensing? Do they bow to the thurifer? Why or why not?

_____

_____

_____

28.   Then the Priest, standing at the side of the altar, washes his hands, saying quietly:

Wash me, O Lord, from my iniquity and cleanse me from my sin.

Then the Priest washes his hands at the side of the altar, a rite in which the desire for interior purification finds expression.

—GIRM, 76

After the prayer _In spiritu humilitatis_ (_With humble spirit and contrite heart_) or after the incensation, the Priest washes his hands standing at the side of the altar and, as the minister pours the water, says quietly, _Lava me, Domine_ (_Wash me, O Lord_).

—GIRM, 145

See also GIRM, 188c.

Background

Servers usually help the priest wash his hands. He goes to the side of the altar, they pour water over his hands into a bowl and offer him a towel. Meanwhile, he says a prayer asking to be cleansed of sin.

The washing of hands took place at different parts of the liturgy before it settled into its present location. The ritual appeared in the seventh and eighth centuries just before the Preparation of the Gifts.[1] A text from Psalm 26:6 ("I wash my hands in innocence") was added by the thirteenth century.[2] It eventually moved into its present location because of the increased use of incensing. It served a practical function of cleaning the hands of the priest after he handled the censer.[3]

Study Group 10, aware of the fluctuations in the history of the handwashing, discussed changing its placement as well as its text. For example, they considered having it at the chair before the preparation of the altar.[4] They also considered keeping it in place, but only when incense was used.[5] In the end, they kept the ritual after preparing and incensing the altar, but changed the text from Psalm 26:6 to Psalm 51:4.

1 Oury, p. 81.
2 Oury, p. 82.

3 Oury, p. 84.
4 Barba, p. 392.
5 Barba, p. 257.

Questions for Discussion and Reflection

1. In your community, where does the washing of hands take place?

_____

_____

_____

2. How do the ministers assist?

_____

_____

_____

3. Are the vessels and the water ample?

_____

_____

_____

29.   Standing at the middle of the altar, facing the people, extending and then joining his hands, he says:

**Pray, brethren (brothers and sisters),
that my sacrifice and yours
may be acceptable to God,
the almighty Father.**

The people rise and reply:

**May the Lord accept the sacrifice at your hands
for the praise and glory of his name,
for our good
and the good of all his holy Church.**

The faithful should stand from the beginning of the Entrance Chant, or while the Priest approaches the altar, until the end of the Collect; for the _Alleluia_ Chant before the Gospel; while the Gospel itself is proclaimed; during the Profession of Faith and the Universal Prayer; and from the invitation, _Orate, fratres_ (_Pray, brethren_), before the Prayer over the Offerings until the end of Mass, except at the places indicated here below. . . .

—GIRM, 43

See also GIRM, 40 and 146.

Background

The priest invites the people to pray for the acceptance of the sacrifice, and they entrust their sacrifice to his hands.

The dialogue began to make its appearance among the Franks in the eighth century, when the priest turned to the other ministers, extended his hands, and humbly asked their prayers that not just their sacrifice but his also would be acceptable. The priest's request and gesture were part of this dialogue from the very beginning.

At first, though, the priest addressed other ministers, not the rest of the assembly.[1] Eventually he began to address the people, and a response was given to them. Remy of Auxerre (+c. 908) said they responded with lines from Psalm 20:2–4, that the Lord would "accept" the sacrifice.[2] This verb endured throughout the use of the 1570 Missal, where servers made the response, and into the 1970 Missal, where the people do.

_____

1   Jungmann 2:82.
2   _Espositio (De divinis officiis liber)_ PL 101:1252; translation PT.

Study Group 10 considered eliminating the invitation and its response to simplify the Preparation of the Gifts; after all, the ideas were already present in the Eucharistic Prayer.[3] Others thought this was not a problem, and that the antiquity and beauty of the dialogue showed roots of participation that should not be lost. After Pope Paul VI called it a "gem," it was retained.[4]

Omitted, however, was the next prayer from the 1570 Missal, addressed to the Trinity. The decision kept the elements of this part of the Mass in high relief: the preparation of the altar, the procession of the gifts, the praising of God for the gifts, the washing of hands, and then a dialogue about the sacrifice soon to happen.

The mention of two sacrifices—that of the priest and that of the people—goes back to the origins of this dialogue. It seems to be rooted in the acknowledgment that the baptized people exercise their priestly ministry by offering sacrifice as well. Each person participates in the one sacrifice.

---

3   Barba, p. 278.
4   Barba, p. 279.

Questions for Discussion and Reflection

1. How well do people respond to the dialogue?

_____

_____

_____

2. Is the collection completed and brought to the altar with the other gifts, or does it continue into the dialogues?

_____

_____

_____

3. The Missal indicates two different times when people stand: from the invitation and after it. When does your community stand? Why?

_____

_____

_____

4. The Missal suggests singing this dialogue. How well would that fit your community?

_____

_____

_____

30. Then the Priest, with hands extended, says the Prayer over the Offerings, at the end of which the people acclaim:

Amen.

Once the offerings have been placed on the altar and the accompanying rites completed, by means of the invitation to pray with the Priest and by means of the Prayer over the Offerings, the Preparation of the Gifts is concluded and preparation made for the Eucharistic Prayer.

At Mass, a single Prayer over the Offerings is said, and it ends with the shorter conclusion, that is: *Through Christ our Lord*. If, however, the Son is mentioned at the end of this prayer, the conclusion is: *Who lives and reigns forever and ever*.

The people, joining in this petition, make the prayer their own by means of the acclamation *Amen*.

—GIRM, 77

See also GIRM, 40 and 146.

Background

The priest offers a Prayer over the Offerings. Usually this asks that they will be pleasing to God, and it may make a reference to the season of the year or the day on the calendar. The people respond "Amen" to make the prayer their own.

Texts for this prayer appear throughout the *Veronese Sacramentary*—and not just a few of them. Examples represent the entire year. This complexity suggests that the prayer was being developed as early as the fourth or fifth centuries. It has gone by different names: "the Prayer over the Offerings" and "the Secret." The *Gelasian Sacramentary* calls it the secret, so the name may have taken root by the middle of the eighth century. By that time, the priest recited the Eucharistic Prayer in a low voice, and that practice may have influenced the way other presidential prayers were recited. It is possible that this prayer was called "secret" because it

was said quietly in anticipation of the style to be used in the Eucharistic Prayer.[1] The word originally meant "to separate" or "seclude," which led to its usage for things in hiding.

The name "secret" was adopted for the 1570 Missal throughout its use, but in 1964, even before the revised Missal was finished, Pope Paul VI asked priests to begin saying the prayer aloud.[2]

This practice remained in force with the finished version of the Preparation of the Gifts. The priest could say all the other texts for this part of the Mass quietly if the congregation was singing something. But the invitation, its response, and the prayer over the offerings were to be said or sung aloud.[3]

---

1 Cabié, *The Church at Prayer* 2:133.
2 Sacred Congregation of Rites (Consilium), Instruction *Inter oecumenici*, DOL 23:48e.
3 Barba, p. 254.

Questions for Discussion and Reflection

1. On what occasion does your priest sing the Prayer over the Offerings? How well do the people sing the "Amen"?

_____

_____

_____

2. The people listen in silence to the prayer before making their response. How can their attention improve?

_____

_____

_____

THE EUCHARISTIC PRAYER

31. Then the Priest begins the Eucharistic Prayer.
     Extending his hands, he says:

The Lord be with you.

The people reply:

And with your spirit.

The Priest, raising his hands, continues:

Lift up your hearts.

The people:

We lift them up to the Lord.

The Priest, with hands extended, adds:

Let us give thanks to the Lord our God.

The people:

It is right and just.

The Priest, with hands extended, continues the Preface.

At the end of the Preface he joins his hands and concludes the Preface with the people, singing or saying aloud:

Holy, Holy, Holy Lord God of hosts.
Heaven and earth are full of your glory.
Hosanna in the highest.
Blessed is he who comes in the name of the Lord
Hosanna in the highest.

Now the center and high point of the entire celebration begins, namely, the Eucharistic Prayer itself, that is, the prayer of thanksgiving and sanctification. The Priest calls upon the people to lift up their hearts towards the Lord in prayer and thanksgiving; he associates the people with himself in the Prayer that he addresses in the name of the entire community to God the Father through Jesus Christ in the Holy Spirit. Furthermore, the meaning of this Prayer is that the whole congregation of the faithful joins with Christ in confessing the great deeds of God and in the offering of Sacrifice. The Eucharistic Prayer requires that everybody listens to it with reverence and in silence.

—GIRM, 78

See also GIRM, 31, 40, 43, 79, 147, 148, 179, 365, and 366.

Background

The Eucharistic Prayer is the "center and high point"[1] of the entire celebration. It offers praise, even as it asks God to change the bread and wine into the Body and Blood of Christ. Long recited quietly by the priest alone, the people are now expected to unite their hearts and minds with the priest as he offers the prayer aloud.

The general style of this prayer has antecedents in Jewish worship.[2] Examples can be found in the Old Testament. When Abraham's servant miraculously discovers Rebekah, the future bride of Isaac, he prays, "Blessed be the LORD, the God of my master Abraham, who has not forsaken his steadfast love and his faithfulness toward my master."[3] Jethro thanked God for ending Israel's slavery: "Blessed be the LORD, who has delivered you from the Egyptians and from Pharaoh."[4] A Eucharistic Prayer is based on the premise that God is to be praised for specific divine actions.

Justin the Martyr tells of the primitive form of the Eucharistic Prayer in the second century:

[The presider] takes [bread and a cup of water and wine mixed together] and offers praise and glory to the Father of the universe, through the name of the Son and of the Holy Spirit and for a considerable time he gives thanks (in Greek: *eucharistian*) that we have been judged worthy of these gifts.

When he has concluded the prayers and thanksgivings, all present give voice to an acclamation by saying: "Amen."[5]

[The presider] offers prayers and thanksgivings, according to his ability, and the people make their assent, proclaiming, "Amen."[6]

The *Apostolic Tradition* attests to a similar practice a century or so later. The text of a Eucharistic Prayer is supplied for a newly ordained Bishop to use.[7] It begins with the dialogue much in the form used today. The opening greeting dates at least to the fourth century. "Lift up your hearts" and "We lift them up to the Lord" are found in

the writings of Cyprian in the fourth century.[8] The third part of the dialogue could date to first-century Jewish and pagan practice, adopted for use in Christian worship.[9] The whole dialogue also appears in the late-fourth-century *Apostolic Constitutions*.[10] Through it the priest and the people prepare themselves for the Eucharistic Prayer, ending with the affirmation that giving thanks to God is the right things to do. The dialogue leads directly into the Preface, which explains why the community gives thanks to God on this occasion.

Justin says the presider prayed "according to his ability," a practice of necessity when liturgical books were few. Today's presiders still pray according to their ability, but using the prescribed texts, which have been formulated by specialists and handed down from one faithful generation to the next.

The Sanctus appears in partial form in the *Apostolic Constitutions*.[11] During the Eucharistic Prayer, after the opening dialogue and a lengthy Preface extolling God for creation and salvation, all the people are invited to sing together with myriads of angels. Their text comes from Isaiah 6:3 (and Revelation 4:8), which has remained throughout the history of the Eucharist as the first part of the Sanctus. The hymn gradually worked its way into the West. Peter Chrysologus (+450) commented on it in one of his sermons.[12] The sixth-century *Liber pontificalis* says the Sanctus was sung in the Roman Church already by the second-century papacy of Sixtus.[13] This is not likely, but it shows that the Roman Church was much familiar with the hymn by the time the *Liber* was written. The second half of the Sanctus, the Benedictus, which quotes Matthew 21:9 and Psalm 118:26, appears in the *Apostolic Constitutions* just before Holy Communion, not with

---

1   GIRM, 78.

2   Klauser, p. 6.

3   Genesis 24:27.

4   Exodus 18:10.

5   *First Apology* 65, cited in CCC, 1345.

6   Ibid., 67, SChr 507:310–311; translation PT.

7   AT 4.

---

8   "Therefore, at the preface set forth before the [eucharistic] prayer, the priest prepares the minds of the faithful saying, 'Lift up your hearts,' so that as the people respond, 'We lift them up to the Lord,' he may admonish that they should think about nothing else but the Lord." *De dominica oratione*, 31, CCL 3A:109; translation PT.

9   Bradshaw et al., *The Apostolic Tradition*, p. 43. Klauser, p. 6.

10   AC 8:12.

11   AC 8:12.

12   *Sermo* 170, PL 52:644.

13   LP I:128.

the Sanctus.[14] The hymn was sung in Gaul by the seventh or eighth century.[15] By the Middle Ages, choirs were singing more elaborate settings of the Sanctus, and the people's participation became more limited. In time, the choir ended the first half of the Sanctus before the elevations, and then took up the Benedictus after them.

The Sanctus probably follows the Preface at every Mass because of the *Apostolic Constitutions*. That Preface praised God for all creation, including the angels, whose song all creation joined. However, other Prefaces did not repeat that content. The Sanctus does not flow neatly from every Preface, but it still gathers into one voice the praise of all in the church, throughout the earth, and above the earth.

The 1570 Missal called for the ringing of bells during the Sanctus, probably to alert the faithful who might otherwise not know that the Eucharistic Prayer was underway. With Mass in the vernacular and the priest facing the people, the 1970 Missal discontinued the ringing of Sanctus bells.

Cyprian implies that the celebrant prayed at least the consecratory texts out loud,[16] but the late-ninth-century *Ordo Romanus V* instructed the Pope to recite the canon quietly.[17] The practice of kneeling for the Eucharistic Prayer did not develop until the thirteenth century.[18] It is possible that the more elaborate singing of the Sanctus led to this practice, in which the presider continued the Eucharistic Prayer under the music that the schola was singing.[19]

In turn, this fed the perception that the Eucharistic Prayer began after the Sanctus. The Preface was still prayed aloud, partly because it varied according to the season and the day. The unchanging part of the Eucharistic Prayer, which followed the Sanctus, became known as the "canon." The title "Roman Canon" appeared on some manuscripts after the hymn.

The 1970 Missal's reform of the Eucharistic Prayer was extraordinary. There was no desire to change the Preface dialogue, which enjoyed such a long history and served the participation of the people. The Sanctus and the Benedictus were

> During the Eucharistic Prayer, after the opening dialogue and a lengthy Preface extolling God for creation and salvation, all the people are invited to sing together with myriads of angels.

restored as a single hymn for priest and people to sing together.[20] Many people, including Pope Paul VI,[21] wanted to leave the Roman Canon unchanged, but as one of several options. Although it was the only Eucharistic Prayer in the Roman Rite for many centuries, others were in use throughout the Church in the East and the West. Three Eucharistic Prayers were added to the Order of Mass, and these were quickly followed by several more for Masses with Children, Masses for Reconciliation, and Masses for Various Needs and Occasions, extending a variety of options in vernacular languages for those unaccustomed to hearing the Eucharistic Prayer at all.

---

14 AC 8:13.
15 Jungmann 2:136.
16 *Epistula* 75:10, CSEL 3:818.
17 OR V:58.
18 Nocent, p. 31.
19 Nocent, p. 33.

20 Barba, p. 362.
21 Barba, p. 177.

Questions for Discussion and Reflection

1. On which occasions does your community sing the Preface Dialogue?

_____

_____

_____

2. On which occasions do you sing the Sanctus?

_____

_____

_____

3. How good is the participation of the people in these parts of the Mass?

_____

_____

_____

4. Are there ever occasions when the choir sings the Sanctus alone? Why?

_____

_____

_____

32.   In all Masses, the Priest celebrant is permitted to sing parts of the Eucharistic Prayer provided with musical notation below . . . especially the principal parts.

In Eucharistic Prayer I, the Roman Canon, the words included in brackets may be omitted.

> . . . It is most appropriate that the Priest sing those parts of the Eucharistic Prayer for which musical notation is provided.
>
> —GIRM, 147
>
> See also GIRM, 40.

Background

The singing of prayers is an ancient practice that highlights their importance. The singing of Eucharistic Prayers is more commonly practiced in the East than the West, but the Roman Rite has always promoted the idea.

The first English translation included chant settings for all the Eucharistic Prayers, and the revised book does as well. However, the 1970 edition of _The Sacramentary_ abbreviated the musical notation for Eucharistic Prayer I, probably because of the length of the prayer. It set the middle part to music, including the Institution narrative, but left recited the parts of the prayer following the Sanctus and preceding the doxology. The revised English translation includes notation for the entire prayer, tacitly proposing that all of it, not part of it, be sung.

Still, the Order of Mass recommends singing at least the "principal parts" of the Eucharistic Prayer. This allows the option of singing a portion of the text. It does not name these principal parts, but surely they are the epiclesis, the Institution narrative, the dialogues, and the acclamations of the people. The acclamations almost demand singing for the integrity of the prayer.

Part of the reform of the Order of Mass was to bracket some lines of Eucharistic Prayer I, making them optional. As will be seen, other measures were considered to reshape the Roman Canon, but these resulted in only light abbreviations.

Questions for Discussion and Reflection

1. On what occasions does the priest in your community sing the Eucharistic Prayer? When might it be appropriate?

_____

_____

_____

2. When using Eucharistic Prayer I, does the priest omit the sections in brackets? On what occasions might it be more appropriate to use these?

_____

_____

_____

33.–82. [Prefaces]

> The *thanksgiving* (expressed especially in the Preface), in which the Priest, in the name of the whole of the holy people, glorifies God the Father and gives thanks to him for the whole work of salvation or for some particular aspect of it, according to the varying day, festivity, or time of year.
>
> —GIRM, 79a
>
> See also GIRM, 148.

Background

The preface is a prayer of thanksgiving that usually names the reasons why the community praises God on this day. The text bridges the dialogue and the Sanctus. It opens with a phrase that echoes the last line of the dialogue, and it ends with a phrase that leads to the Sanctus.

Early versions of the Eucharistic Prayer include an opening thanksgiving of this kind. Examples can be found in third to fourth-century texts such as the *Apostolic Tradition*,[1] the prayer of Ambrose,[2] and the one in the *Apostolic Constitutions*.[3]

As prayers became more formulaic, the Preface resisted, becoming a changeable text. By the fifth-century *Veronese Sacramentary*, a different Preface appears on the page for almost every day of the year. In the sixth-century Pope Vigilius explained the practice:

> We do not have a different set of prayers for the celebration of masses of a particular season or feast, but always use the same text in consecrating the gifts offered to God. But whenever we celebrate the feasts of Easter, the Ascension of the Lord, Pentecost, Epiphany, or the saints of God, we add special paragraphs proper to the day.[4]

Although the Preface was integral to the Eucharistic Prayer from the beginning, its significance was lost during the Middle Ages. Rabanus Maurus (+856) said the prayer of consecration began after the Sanctus.[5] As will be seen, the Missal customarily included a page carrying the image of the Crucifixion, which visually separated the Preface from the Eucharistic Prayer.[6]

---

1 AT 4.
2 *De sacramentis* 4:56.
3 AC 8:12.

4 *Epistula* 2:5, PL 69:18; translation PT.
5 PL 112:1182.
6 See the first paragraph on page 71.

The number of Prefaces diminished during the Middle Ages.[7] The few Prefaces that appeared in the 1474 Missal were expanded to fifteen in the 1570 Missal. Study Group 10 wanted to expand the number of Prefaces, in keeping with the earlier Roman tradition.[8] As a result, the third edition of *The Roman Missal* now has 99 Prefaces in its index. Most of these are based on ones from an earlier tradition.

---

7 Botte and Mohrmann, p. 25.

8 Barba, p. 476.

Questions for Discussion and Reflection

1. Over the course of the year, does your community get to hear a wide variety of Prefaces?

_____

_____

_____

2. How do you decide which Preface will be offered?

_____

_____

_____

3. Preaching may treat the texts of the Mass. How often does a homily refer to a Preface?

_____

_____

_____

EUCHARISTIC PRAYER I (THE ROMAN CANON)

83. V. The Lord be with you.
     R. And with your spirit.

     V. Lift up your hearts.
     R. We lift them up to the Lord.

     V. Let us give thanks to the Lord our God.
     R. It is right and just.

Then follows the Preface to be used in accord with the rubrics, which concludes:

Holy, Holy, Holy Lord God of hosts.
Heaven and earth are full of your glory.
Hosanna in the highest.
Blessed is he who comes in the name of the Lord.
Hosanna in the highest.

Eucharistic Prayer I, or the Roman Canon, which may always be used, is especially suited for use on days to which a proper text for the *Communicantes* (*In communion with those whose memory we venerate*) is assigned or in Masses endowed with a proper form of the *Hanc ígitur* (*Therefore, Lord, we pray*) and also in the celebrations of the Apostles and of the Saints mentioned in the Prayer itself; likewise it is especially suited for use on Sundays, unless for pastoral reasons Eucharistic Prayer III is preferred.

—GIRM, 365a

See also GIRM, 147.

Background

The Roman Canon is the first Eucharistic Prayer in the Order of Mass. For many centuries, it was the only one.

The word "canon" refers to its fixed nature. This kind of prayer is often called an "anaphora," which means "offering." Indeed, "we offer you" is a key phrase in the Roman Canon. But the Order of Mass now calls this a "Eucharistic Prayer"—a prayer of thanksgiving. The word "canon" properly applies only to Eucharistic Prayer I because of its time as the only canonical Eucharistic Prayer in the Roman Rite. But speaking generically of all the options for this part of the Mass, they are more properly called Eucharistic Prayers.[1]

The earliest extant version of this particular prayer comes from a work on the sacraments by Ambrose of Milan (+397).

> Acknowledge this oblation, make it spiritual and acceptable, for it is a figure of the body and blood of our Lord Jesus Christ. On the day before he was to suffer, he took bread in his holy hands, looked to heaven, to you, holy Father, almighty, eternal God, giving thanks, he said the blessing, broke, and passed it broken to the apostles and his disciples, saying, "Take this, all of you, and consume of it, for this is my body, which will be broken for many." Take note. Similarly also, on the day before he was to suffer, when supper was ended, he took the chalice, looked to heaven, to you, holy Father, almighty, eternal God, giving thanks, he said the blessing, and passed it to the apostles and his disciples, saying, "Take this, all of you, and drink from it, for this is my blood." . . . [Know then how great is this sacrament. See what he says: "As often as you shall do this, so often will you do a commemoration of me, until I come again."] Therefore, as we celebrate the memorial of his most glorious passion and resurrection from the dead and ascension into heaven, we offer you this spotless victim, a spiritual sacrifice, an unbloody victim, this holy bread and the chalice of eternal life. And we ask and pray that you receive this offering upon your altar on high through the hands of your angels, just as you were pleased to receive the gifts of your servant Abel the just, the sacrifice of Abraham, our father in faith, and the offering of the high priest Melchizedek.[2]

The primitive form of the prayer is evident. The dialogue, the Preface, and the Sanctus are missing. The opening flows more smoothly without its first group of intercessions. Saints are not listed. There is no epiclesis and no elevation. Yet from this initial form, the Roman Canon evolved. It has not changed significantly

> The word "canon" refers to its fixed nature. This kind of prayer is often called an "anaphora," which means "offering."

since the time of Gregory the Great (+604),[3] and it appears in complete form in the *Gelasian Sacramentary* of the mid-eighth century, probably retaining the text that Gregory knew.[4] Here the word "canon" appears at the head of the entire prayer, not after the Sanctus. By the ninth century, the use of the periodic "Amens" of the canon was spreading rapidly.[5] The canon was introduced into England in the seventh century, into Frankish territory in the eighth, into Spain in the eleventh, and into Celtic countries from the ninth to the twelfth century.[6]

Although the prayer remained substantially the same throughout various cultures and times, it always enjoyed some fluctuation and development. Certain elements were changeable depending on the season of the year or the feast celebrated. Sections of the prayer expanded. Knowing this history, Study Group 10 considered additional changes to the prayer for the 1970 Missal.[7]

The group proposed three ways of handling the Roman Canon. The first made the fewest changes, eliminating a phrase about those for whom the prayer is offered, as well as the periodic "Amens." The second shortened and combined the two groups of intercessions, as well as the two groups of saints, retaining only the names of the biblical saints. The third proposal resembled the second except that it combined

---

1 Barba, pp. 488, 520, and 521.

2 *De sacramentis* 4:5–6; translation PT.
3 *Letter to John of Syracuse* PL 77:957.
4 Gelasian 1242–1255.
5 Botte and Mohrmann, p. 24.
6 Mazza, p. 53.
7 Barba, p. 478.

the prayers for the living and the dead to a position near the end of the prayer. This would have streamlined the text between the Sanctus and the Institution narrative, resembling its original form in Ambrose.[8] In the end, the group decided not to change the Roman Canon in these ways. It preserved the text, but expanded the number of Eucharistic Prayers, according to other traditional designs.[9]

Today, the Roman Canon holds a privileged position as the first Eucharistic Prayer of the Order of Mass. It is recommended on days when special insertions can be made to it, and when different Prefaces can be used, such as Sundays during the seasons of the year.

---

8 Barba, pp. 478–479.

9 Barba, p. 487.

Questions for Discussion and Reflection

1. On which occasions does your community use Eucharistic Prayer I?

_____

_____

_____

2. How often is it prayed on Sundays?

_____

_____

_____

3. When might be appropriate occasions for its use?

_____

_____

_____

84.   The Priest, with hands extended, says:

To you, therefore, most merciful Father,
we make humble prayer and petition
through Jesus Christ, your Son, our Lord:

He joins his hands and says

that you accept

He makes the Sign of the Cross once over the bread and chalice together, saying:

and bless ✛ these gifts, these offerings,
these holy and unblemished sacrifices,

The *intercessions*, by which expression is given to the fact that the Eucharist is celebrated in communion with the whole Church, of both heaven and of earth, and that the oblation is made for her and for all her members, living and dead, who are called to participate in the redemption and salvation purchased by the Body and Blood of Christ.

—GIRM, 79g

See also GIRM, 79c, 149, and 219.

With hands extended, he continues:

which we offer you firstly
for your holy catholic Church.
Be pleased to grant her peace,
to guard, unite and govern her
throughout the whole world,
together with your servant N. our Pope
and N. our Bishop,*
and all those who, holding to the truth,
hand on the catholic and apostolic faith.

---

* Mention may be made here of the Coadjutor Bishop, or Auxiliary Bishops, as noted in the *General Instruction of the Roman Missal,* no. 149.

Background

Following the Sanctus, the priest asks God to accept the offerings, and to grant peace to the Church. Given the structure of the other Eucharistic Prayers, the appearance of an intercession so soon in the prayer may surprise, but this prayer follows a tradition originating in Alexandria, Egypt, which organizes an anaphora this way. This section did not appear in the version recorded by Ambrose, but intercessions before the consecration may have been added before the time of Leo the Great (+461).[1]

In Latin, this section is known by its first two words, *Te igitur.* The first letter of the first word inspired iconographers to decorate this text with a crucifix. Eventually, an image of the Crucifixion took over a page of its own, making a visual cue to the start of the canon. Today, the heading "Eucharistic Prayer I" and "Roman Canon" surmount the dialogue, lest anyone think that the Eucharistic Prayer begins here. Still, the revised English translation has successfully started this section with a word that begins with a capital T, making it possible again to decorate the text in the traditional way.

In some anaphoras, the section following the Sanctus makes a direct allusion back to it, but this one does not. The earliest form of Eucharistic Prayer I predates the inclusion of the Sanctus. This section was added later, but it still made no reference to the hymn.

It does begin with the word "therefore," but the next lines do not logically follow what precedes. The word perhaps attempts to link this section to the Sanctus, as if the holiness of God leads to a petition. After all, God is the one to whom the prayer is addressed, so the petition is "therefore" made humbly, and made through Jesus, the one who comes in the name of the Lord.

The first English translation of this section began, "We come to you, Father, with praise and thanksgiving." This mentioned the community before naming God, an inversion of priorities that the revision corrects. It also inserted the expression "with praise and thanksgiving," a good theological interpretation of the purpose of a Eucharistic Prayer, but a phrase that this particular anaphora had never said.

The priest asks God to bless the gifts, and he makes a single Sign of the Cross over the bread and the chalice. The 1970 Missal simplified this action, which required three crosses even in the 1474 Missal. The blessing of the gifts bears some resemblance to an epiclesis, but Eucharistic Prayer I makes no explicit appeal for the coming of the Holy Spirit as all the other Eucharistic Prayers do.

God is asked to bless "gifts," "offerings," and "sacrifices." These are essentially synonyms, but a similar text in another ancient anaphora distinguishes them as gifts for the deceased, offerings for the living, and the sacrifices that pertain

---

1   Botte and Mohrmann, p. 22.

to this particular Eucharist.[2] Already the gifts are called "holy" and "unblemished" even though the consecration has not yet taken place. These words probably mean the appropriateness of the gifts that have been presented.

The specific petition for the Church is for peace. The other verbs seem to describe how that peace will come: God will "guard, unite and govern" the Church. Among the members, the Pope and Bishop are singled out by name. Originally, the Roman Canon would have prayed for the local Bishop, who was also the Pope. As the canon was used more broadly, the name of the local Bishop would have been added. Alcuin (+804) broadened the petition to include all those who hand on the faith,[3] implying that the faithfulness of all the Church's leaders would achieve the unity that the prayer

2 Mazza, p. 59.
3 Botte and Mohrmann, p. 24.

desires. In some medieval traditions, the priest also said the name of the civic ruler, probably because there was little distinction between the local governance of Church and State.

The prayer commends to God only the Christian faithful. When it was composed, those outside the Church could have been remembered in the prayer of the faithful, but not in the Eucharistic Prayer.

Again, to those familiar with eucharistic prayers that put the petitions near the end, it is surprising to see an explicit intercession for the peace of the Church so early in this one. However, by praying for the Church and the hierarchy, the prayer connects the offering with the people who make it. The offerings are a symbol of the people. When asking God to accept the bread and wine that are holy and unblemished, the priest implies that the Church could be described in the same way.

Questions for Discussion and Reflection

1. How does this petition differ from the Prayer of the Faithful in your community? Do you typically pray for the Pope and the local Bishop in both parts of the Mass?

_____

_____

_____

2. Are other bishops mentioned? Who and why?

_____

_____

_____

3. How does the priest hold his hands while he prays this section? How clear is his gesture when he makes the Sign of the Cross?

_____

_____

_____

85. Commemoration of the Living.

Remember, Lord, your servants N. and N.

The Priest joins his hands and prays briefly for those for whom he intends to pray.

Then, with hands extended, he continues:

and all gathered here,
whose faith and devotion are known to you.
For them, we offer you this sacrifice of praise
or they offer it for themselves
and all who are dear to them:
for the redemption of their souls,
in hope of health and well-being,
and paying their homage to you,
the eternal God, living and true.

> . . . For the Celebration of the Eucharist is the action of the whole Church, and in it each one should carry out solely but totally that which pertains to him, in virtue of the place of each within the People of God . . .
>
> —GIRM, 5
>
> See also GIRM, 2.

Background

The prayer continues with the commemoration of the living; in Latin, the *Memento, Domine*. As the previous section asked God to accept the offering as well as the Church that makes it, so this section further specifies the members of the community at prayer. The priest pauses to pray specifically for certain living members of the community, and for all who have gathered for worship. On their behalf he offers this sacrifice. The connection between the previous section, which asked God to accept the offerings, and this one, which continues to name the offerers, is attested by Pope Innocent I (+417): "Above all, the offerings are to be recommended and then the names of those who have supplied the offerings are to be read."[1]

The members are called "servants," a word that may link them to Moses and Jesus.[2] The Book of Joshua, for example, frequently calls Moses the servant of the Lord.[3] Jesus took the role of a servant when he washed the feet of the disciples;[4] indeed, he said he came among them as one who serves.[5]

The specific names are probably those who have made a material offering for the sacrifice at hand. Jerome (+420) mentioned the practice. "Then the names of those offering are recited

> The action is called a "sacrifice of praise," perhaps a reference to Psalm 50:23. But the complete phrase also mentions other purposes beyond praise: redemption, and the hope of health.

publicly, and the ransom for sinners turns into their commendation."[6] Alcuin added the phrase "for them we offer you," and the lines seem to indicate two possibilities: either those who made the offering are absent, or they are present. If they are absent, the priest prays on their behalf; if present, they offer the sacrifice themselves.

This translation uses "all gathered here" instead of the more literal "all standing here" for the Latin words *"omnium circumstantium."* In the United States of America people kneel for this part of the Eucharistic Prayer; in most other countries they stand.

The action is called a "sacrifice of praise," perhaps a reference to Psalm 50:23. But the complete phrase also mentions other purposes

---

1   *Letter to Decentius of Gubbio*, PL 20:553–554; translation PT.

2   Mazza, pp. 298–299.

3   See Joshua 1:13, 15; 8:31, 33; and 11:12.

4   See John 13:3–16.

5   See Luke 22:27.

6   *In Hieremiam Propheticam* 2:108, CCL 74:116; tra.

beyond praise: redemption, and the hope of health. This fits with the traditional threefold purposes of sacrifice: praise, atonement, and petition.[7] Prayer for the hope of salvation echoes 1 Thessalonians 5:8 and Romans 8:24, "in hope we are saved."

When Study Group 10 prepared the revision of the Roman Canon, members considered displacing this entire section to the end of the prayer, where petition is made for the dead.[8] The idea was to group the petitions together after the consecration, where they could be made as a unit. In the end, though, no change was made to the structure of Eucharistic Prayer I. Its long pedigree argued for keeping the prayer intact, rather than rearranging its parts.

---

7 Fortiscue, p. 330.

8 Barba, p. 381.

Questions for Discussion and Reflection

1. How does the priest speak the first line of this section? Does he pause to pray privately? Does he mention names aloud? Would that be appropriate?

_____

_____

_____

2. Again, do these intercessions differ from those your community composes for the Prayer of the Faithful? How?

_____

_____

_____

3. During scrutiny rites and at baptisms, the priest may speak aloud the names of the godparents at this point of Eucharistic Prayer I. Does this ever happen in your community?

_____

_____

_____

86.   Within the Action.

In communion with those whose memory we venerate,
especially the glorious ever-Virgin Mary,
Mother of our God and Lord, Jesus Christ,
✠ and blessed Joseph, her Spouse,
your blessed Apostles and Martyrs,
Peter and Paul, Andrew,
(James, John,
Thomas, James, Philip,
Bartholomew, Matthew,
Simon and Jude;

In the earthly Liturgy, the Church participates, by a foretaste, in that heavenly Liturgy which is celebrated in the holy city of Jerusalem, toward which she journeys as a pilgrim, and where Christ is seated at the right hand of God; and by venerating the memory of the Saints, she hopes one day to have some share and fellowship with them.

—GIRM, 318

See also GIRM, 365a.

Linus, Cletus, Clement, Sixtus,
Cornelius, Cyprian,
Lawrence, Chrysogonus,
John and Paul,
Cosmas and Damian)
and all your Saints;
we ask that through their merits and prayers,
in all things we may be defended
by your protecting help.
(Through Christ our Lord. Amen.)

Background

Ultimately, this section prays that God will defend the Church with protecting help. The request is made, however, in communion with saints, and the listing of their names gives this section, the *Communicantes*, its identity. A second characteristic, though, accounts for the placement of this section. This part of the prayer may be amplified on special days of celebration, giving it a function similar to the Preface, which may elaborate the meaning of the day on the calendar. For this reason, the section has another Latin title, *Infra actionem,* which alerts the priest that the allusion to the liturgical day occurs "within the act" of the Eucharistic Prayer, and not just at some other point of the Mass. This section, although not part of the earliest evidence of this canon, was under development by the fifth century.[1]

Sample insertions appear in the *Verona, Gregorian,* and *Gelasian Sacramentaries.* They have changed very little in their entire history, so even though they were added after the earliest version of the canon, they have been retained and honored for their antiquity. To this day there are proper insertions for Christmas and its octave, the epiphany, Easter and its octave, the Ascension, and Pentecost. All these appear in the Order of Mass. The special insert for Holy Thursday is found among the texts for that day, where all of Eucharistic Prayer I appears again. There is no logical reason why an allusion to a solemnity occurs in this place, where the saints are mentioned and God's protection is sought.

But the practice is retained because of the age of the custom.

Among the saints, Mary appropriately heads the list. She is remembered under the title "Mother of God." The Council of Ephesus (431) assigned her that title, and the canon embraced it shortly after that, probably to unify the belief of the Church in the deity of Jesus and the role of Mary.

> Among the saints, Mary appropriately heads the list. She is remembered under the title "Mother of God."

Pope John XXIII added Joseph to the list immediately after Mary. The decree was dated November 13, 1962,[2] just before the close of the first session of the Second Vatican Council. It sent a signal to those debating liturgical changes that the Roman Canon could change again as it had many times over the centuries. Joseph was the baptismal patron of Giuseppe Roncalli, who became John XXIII. Joseph was also patron of a number of Eastern European countries under communism at that time.

The rest of the saints are grouped in twelves. The list of the apostles omits Judas, of course, but inserts Paul next to Peter, the founders of the Church of Rome. The precise sequence of names does not match the list in any one of the Gospel accounts. The names of the apostles are followed by twelve male martyrs honored by the Roman Church. The first six are Bishops. The last of these, Cyprian, oversaw an African church; hence, he is the only non-Roman in the half-dozen, and the only non-Pope in this first list of martyrs. The next two are clerics, and the

1   Jungmann 2:173.

2   AAS 54 (1962):873.

last four are laymen.[3] The list enjoyed some fluctuation over the years; for example, some churches in medieval Gaul included the local saints Hilary and Martin.[4]

This section asks God to grant protection "through [the] merits and prayers" of the saints. The original phrase is an ablative absolute, which would permit a translation using other prepositions such as "with," "by," or "at." The Catholic Church has long stressed the intercessory role of the saints, even though some other Christian bodies do not embrace it. As will be seen, all the other Eucharistic Prayers of the current rite reduced the number of saints mentioned and avoided the controversial issue of intercession, as a nod to ecumenism.

Some members of Study Group 10 expressed a desire to revise the list of saints in Eucharistic Prayer I.[5] This would have allowed a list more representative of the Church's martyrs from different areas and times. Others suggested abbreviating and combining this list with the one after

the consecration.[6] In the end, the only change made the names of most of the saints optional.

This section concludes with a short doxology ("through Christ our Lord"), the first of many that also became optional.[7] The doxology began to appear in the early Middle Ages, and here it seems to draw together the three sections of the prayer immediately following the Sanctus. God is asked to accept the gift, to unite the Church, and to protect the Church through the prayers of the saints. The "Amen" that concludes the doxology began to appear in the ninth century, and there is some late evidence that the faithful said it aloud. But it was probably added to the priest's lines as an automatic conclusion, and did not originally involve an acclamation by the people.[8]

Three of these brief doxologies that interleave the traditional Roman Canon ended "through the same Christ our Lord," and this was one of them. The revision of the text for the 1970 Missal omitted the Latin word "eundem" ("the same") in all these instances.

---

3 Jungmann, 2:172-173.
4 Cabié, *The Church at Prayer,* 2:164.
5 Barba, p. 362.

6 Barba, p. 427.
7 Barba, p. 426.
8 Jungmann, 2:179.

Questions for Discussion and Reflection

1. On what occasions does your community hear the special inserts of the *Communicantes*? Or is Eucharistic Prayer I not used on those occasions?

_____

_____

_____

2. On which occasions do you hear the entire list of saints in this section? When might it seem more appropriate?

_____

_____

_____

87. With hands extended, the Priest continues:

Therefore, Lord, we pray:
graciously accept this oblation of our service,
that of your whole family;
order our days in your peace,
and command that we be delivered from eternal
    damnation
and counted among the flock of those you have chosen.

        He joins his hands.

(Through Christ our Lord. Amen.)

Moreover, in order that such a celebration may correspond more fully to the prescriptions and spirit of the Sacred Liturgy, and also in order that its pastoral effectiveness be enhanced, certain accommodations and adaptations are set out in this General Instruction and in the Order of Mass.

—GIRM, 23

See also GIRM, 79g.

Background

This section, in Latin called the *Hanc igitur*, asks God to accept the service of the Church in return for peace and redemption. Its purpose so resembles the section following the Sanctus that the reason for its insertion is hard to see. It seems to be here because it can expand at those celebrations permitting a mention of individuals marking a special occasion.

The Order of Mass includes the version that may be used for Easter and its Octave. It is particularly useful when those baptized at Easter are present for the Eucharist. In the early Church, the Octave of Easter was the primary occasion for mystagogical catechesis. The Bishop presided over the assembly that included the newly baptized, and he continued their formation with a series of homilies. The practice is no longer observed, but the adapted *Hanc igitur* has remained. Additional variations can be found in ritual Masses, such as those for the Scrutinies, Baptism, Confirmation, Ordination, and Marriage. The one for Holy Thursday, which mentions Jesus rather than any other individuals, first appeared in the *Gregorian Sacramentary*, and has remained unchanged for nearly 1,500 years.[1]

The *Veronese Sacramentary* has over fifty variations of the *Hanc igitur*, but it is not clear when they were used. It is possible that this section developed as a separate prayer for special occasions, and then was brought into the canon with a generic formula. The *Liber pontificalis* says Gregory the Great added the final words of the section, beginning with "order our days in your peace," perhaps to limit the variations of this prayer by summarizing their purpose into one.[2]

This may also explain why the word "therefore" appears at the start of this section. The content does not logically flow from what precedes, so it may have served some other original purpose in the *Veronese Sacramentary*, and "therefore" remained when it was brought into the Roman Canon.

The independent origins of the *Hanc igitur* can also be seen in the doxology and Amen that conclude it. These have been made optional in the 1970 Missal.

The study group preparing the 1970 Missal considered eliminating the *Hanc igitur* from the Eucharistic Prayer at Masses without one of its special formulations.[3] In the end, though, the structure of the Roman Canon was not changed in order to preserve its various parts.

1   Anthony Ward, "Euchology for the Mass 'In Cena Domini' of the 2000 *Missale Romanum,*" *Notitiae* 507–508 (December 2008, 11–12): 631.

2   Mazza, p. 67.

3   Barba, p. 427.

Questions for Discussion and Reflection

1. In your community, do you hear the special versions of the *Hanc igitur* on Holy Thursday, Octave of Easter, and ritual Masses such as marriage? Or do you use some other Eucharistic Prayer on those occasions?

_____

_____

_____

2. How does the presider handle the optional doxology? Why does he include or exclude it?

_____

_____

_____

88.   Holding his hands extended over the offerings, he says:

Be pleased, O God, we pray,
to bless, acknowledge,
and approve this offering in every respect;
make it spiritual and acceptable,
so that it may become for us
the Body and Blood of your most beloved Son,
our Lord Jesus Christ.

He joins his hands.

> The gestures and bodily posture of both the Priest, the Deacon, and the ministers, and also of the people, must be conducive to making the entire celebration resplendent with beauty and noble simplicity, to making clear the true and full meaning of its different parts, and to fostering the participation of all . . . .
>
> —GIRM, 42

Background

In this section, the *Quam oblationem*, the priest extends his hands over the offerings and asks

The current prayer, however, assumes that the consecration of the elements follows with the words of institution, so the verb has changed: "that it may become" the Body and Blood of Christ.

God to make them spiritual, so that they may become the Body and Blood of Jesus Christ. It is part of the earliest known version of the canon, the section with which Ambrose begins his account of this Eucharistic Prayer.

The *Quam oblationem* has taken three elements from Ambrose ("acknowledge," "make it spiritual and acceptable") and joined them to three elements from the Mozarabic liturgy of about the same period ("bless," "approve," and "make it spiritual"). Probably the original key

phrase is the one that is common to both sources: "make it spiritual."[1] This is likely an allusion to the "spiritual milk" that newborn Christians crave,[2] and to the "spiritual worship" that Christians offer when they present their bodies to God as a sacrifice.[3]

The purpose of this section in Ambrose is very different from the one today. Ambrose implies that the bread and wine are already the Body and Blood of Christ. He calls the sacrifice a "figure," or better, a "sacrament." He is asking God to accept the sacrifice of what already is. The current prayer, however, assumes that the consecration of the

---

1   Botte and Mohrmann, p. 117.
2   1 Peter 2:2.
3   See Romans 12:1. See also the collect for the Fourth Sunday in Ordinary Time.

elements follows with the words of institution, so the verb has changed: "that it may become" the Body and Blood of Christ.[4] Some have argued that this constitutes an epiclesis, but a proper epiclesis would explicitly mention the Holy Spirit, and this text does not.

The priest stretches his hands over the offerings. He is not to make the Sign of the Cross again. This gesture, unknown in the original versions of the Roman Canon, was added quite late. In fact, the 1570 Missal instructed the priest to extend his hands over the offerings for the previous section, the *Hanc igitur*. During this section he made a series of five Signs of the Cross over the elements. Those have been eliminated, and the extension of his hands over the offerings has been moved to the *Quam oblationem*.

---

4   Mazza, p. 68–72.

Questions for Discussion and Reflection

1. How does the priest make the gesture over the elements? Is it deliberate?

_____

_____

_____

2. How does it connect to the words of this section?

_____

_____

_____

89.   In the formulas that follow, the words of the Lord should be pronounced clearly and distinctly, as the nature of these words requires.

On the day before he was to suffer,

> He takes the bread
> and, holding it slightly raised above the altar, continues:

he took bread in his holy and venerable hands,

> He raises his eyes.

and with eyes raised to heaven
to you, O God, his almighty Father,
giving you thanks he said the blessing,
broke the bread
and gave it to his disciples, saying:

Moreover, the wondrous mystery of the real presence of the Lord under the Eucharistic species, confirmed by the Second Vatican Council and other teachings of the Church's Magisterium in the same sense and with the same doctrine as the Council of Trent proposed that it must be believed, is proclaimed in the celebration of the Mass, not only by the very words of consecration by which Christ is rendered present through transubstantiation, but also with a sense and a demonstration of the greatest reverence and adoration which strives for realization in the Eucharistic liturgy. . . .

—GIRM, 3

See also GIRM, 1 and 274.

He bows slightly.

Take this, all of you, and eat of it,
For this is my Body
Which will be given up for you.

He shows the consecrated host to the people, places it again on the paten, and genuflects in adoration.

Background

The priest recounts the events of the Last Supper, holding the bread and cup as Jesus did, and repeating the words that he said. The Roman Catholic Church understands these to be the words of consecration, in which the bread and wine become the Body and Blood of Christ.

Grammatically, this whole section in Latin is a subordinate clause modifying "Jesus Christ" at the end of the previous section. The English translation has rendered it as an independent clause for clarity of enunciation and comprehension.

The section (*Qui pridie*) is based on four passages from the New Testament.[1] The four verbs appear in all these passages ("took," "giving thanks," "broke," and "gave"), though Matthew and Mark use "bless" instead of "give thanks." The Greek word for giving thanks is the origin of the word "eucharist," which gives its name to the entire ritual. All four scripture passages include the words, "This is my body," but Luke and Paul add the phrase "for you."

This section is a staple in anaphoras. The *Didache* (c. 100) has prayers of thanksgiving over the cup and the bread, though they do not repeat the words of Jesus.[2] A similar text appears in the *Apostolic Tradition*, where Jesus invites the disciples to eat his body, which (not the bread) will be broken for them.[3] The parallel section in the *Apostolic Constitutions* is very similar to the one in the Roman Canon,[4] which of course derives from the work of Ambrose. However, the earliest anaphoras are not all alike, even in this significant part of the prayer. Famously, the third-century Assyrian and Chaldean Eucharistic Prayer of Addai and Mari does not have the Institution narrative at all, yet the entire prayer consecrates.[5]

Some non-biblical elements have entered the canon. Jesus' hands are "holy and venerable," and his eyes are "raised to heaven." According to John, Jesus raised his eyes for his prayer to the Father at the Last Supper,[6] but the other Gospel accounts do not mention this.

The elevations of the consecrated bread and chalice were added to the liturgy in the twelfth and thirteenth centuries, when theologians in Paris were disputing whether the bread became the Body of Christ with the pertinent words of Jesus, or only after the wine was also consecrated. To affirm the real presence of Christ in the bread immediately upon the repetition of Jesus' words, the elevation was added to the Mass. About a century later, the priest began to elevate the chalice as well.[7] The first reference to ringing a bell appeared at about the same time,[8] as did the optional incensations.[9] The elevation was added to show the host to the people so that they could adore it. The elevations were not adopted universally until the 1570 Missal, which also called for the priest to genuflect before and after each one. This collection of ritual elements around the words of Jesus probably resulted from a reaction to the denial of the real presence by some Protestant groups. It effectively changed the purpose of the Eucharistic Prayer for the congregation. By this time, people received Holy Communion infrequently, so the Eucharistic Prayer, which began as a prayer of thanksgiving articulated by the priest on behalf of the whole community

1   See Matthew 26:26; Mark 14:22; Luke 22:19; 1 Corinthians 11:23–24.

2   *Didache* 9:2–3.

3   AT 4:9.

4   AC 8:12.

5   Robert F. Taft, SJ, "Mass without the Consecration?" *America* 188/16 (May 12, 2003):7–11.

6   See John 17:1.

7   Nocent, p. 35.

8   Cabié, *History of the Mass*, p. 77.

9   Fortiscue, p. 344.

became a prayer that framed the consecration and elevation of the sacred elements for the purpose of adoration by people who would not be receiving Holy Communion at the Mass.

Study Group 10 made very few changes here. Its members simplified the actions by eliminating two genuflections[10] and making the ringing of bells optional[11] because they were no longer required to draw the attention of the people to the consecration. Members discussed changing the genuflections to a profound bow, partly out of a concern that multiple genuflections were interrupting the narrative flow of the text, and partly because of the infirmity of elderly priests, who found it difficult to genuflect.[12]

To the words of Jesus, the study group added the phrase, "which will be given up for you." This directly quotes Luke's account of the Gospel, but did not appear in the Missal prior to 1970. The addition was intended to strengthen the sacrificial nature of the institution of the Eucharist.[13] Although the group did not wish to alter the text of the Roman Canon, it did so in this instance to unify its Institution narrative with that of the other Eucharistic Prayers.

The rubric calls for the priest to show the host to the people. Before the 1970 Missal,

when he presided with his back to the people, he had to raise the host over his head for them to see it. Now he may use a lower gesture to distinguish this showing from the lifting of the elements at the end of the Eucharistic Prayer.

The Institution narrative began as a subordinate clause. Its purpose was to name the main reason why the community was asking God to make the offering spiritual. It served an anamnetic role within the Eucharistic Prayer, listing among the great works of God the institution of the Eucharist and the command to do this in memory of Jesus. However, it attracted certain dramatic features (the priest taking the elements from the altar in imitation of the actions of Jesus, while repeating the words of Jesus, words that the Catholic Church declares are consecratory), as well as some devotional features (bowing while reciting the text, raising the consecrated elements, ringing bells, and swinging incense) to encourage the adoration of the faithful. In practice, some priests look at the people while saying the text, adding another dramatic feature, while others extend the genuflections into longer periods of adoration. The Institution narrative consecrates, and the moment deserves devout recognition, but structurally this section of the Eucharistic Prayer is praising the Father more than it imitates Jesus or evokes Eucharistic Adoration.

---

10 Barba, p. 625.
11 See GIRM, 150.
12 Barba, p. 426.
13 Barba, p. 557.

Questions for Discussion and Reflection

1. How does your community experience the consecration of the bread? Does the priest say the words distinctly?

_____

_____

_____

2. Are the priests's gestures clear: showing the consecrated bread, and genuflecting?

_____

_____

_____

3. The priest is to "show" the bread to the people. This is different from "taking" the bread during the Preparation of the Gifts and "lifting" it at the end of the Eucharistic Prayer. How should these gestures be differentiated so that their meaning is clear?

_____

_____

_____

4. When the priest shows the bread, do the people look at it? Or do they bow their heads?

_____

_____

_____

90.   After this, the Priest continues:

In a similar way, when supper was ended,

He takes the chalice
and, holding it slightly raised above the altar, continues:

he took this precious chalice in his holy and venerable hands, and once more giving you thanks, he said the blessing and gave the chalice to his disciples, saying:

He bows slightly.

TAKE THIS, ALL OF YOU, AND DRINK FROM IT, FOR THIS IS THE CHALICE OF MY BLOOD, THE BLOOD OF THE NEW AND ETERNAL COVENANT, WHICH WILL BE POURED OUT FOR YOU AND FOR MANY FOR THE FORGIVENESS OF SINS.

DO THIS IN MEMORY OF ME.

He shows the chalice to the people, places it on the corporal, and genuflects in adoration.

. . . For Christ took the bread and the chalice, gave thanks, broke the bread and gave it to his disciples, saying: Take, eat and drink: this is my Body; this is the chalice of my Blood. Do this in memory of me. Hence, the Church has arranged the entire celebration of the Liturgy of the Eucharist in parts corresponding to precisely these words and actions of Christ, ...

—GIRM, 72

See also GIRM, 150 and 179.

Background

The priest continues the story of the Last Supper by stating the words and actions of Jesus concerning the cup. The Roman Catholic Church considers these to be the words for the consecration of the wine.

The section is based on four biblical passages.[1] Together with the words for the consecration of the bread, these have been significant lines in the history of eucharistic prayers. The *Didache* alludes to them, the *Apostolic Tradition* and *Apostolic Constitutions* have them. So does Ambrose.

1   See Matthew 26:27–28; Mark 14:23–24; Luke 22:20; and 1 Corinthians 11:25.

Up to the Missal of the Second Vatican Council, the words for the consecration of the cup included the expression, "the mystery of faith." The study group raised questions about this because these words are not biblical, they appear only in the Roman tradition, the meaning was not clear, the origin and precise sense were disputed, and they interrupt the sentence, making the last part more difficult to understand.[2] The words were removed from the words of institution, but given new life as the introduction to the Memorial Acclamation in the next section of the prayer.

Jesus' words, "Do this in memory of me," do not appear in Matthew and Mark. They do appear in Luke and 1 Corinthians, but he says them after the bread and again after the cup in Paul, and only after the *bread* in Luke. The Institution Narrative of the Eucharistic Prayer is not meant to be a direct rendering of the biblical evidence, but to faithfully hand on the tradition. Here the command to "do this" draws the section to a more exhortative close.

Similarly, the word "chalice" appears in Luke and 1 Corinthians, but not in Matthew and Mark, where Jesus calls the wine "my blood of the covenant." In the discourse on the bread of life, Jesus says that those who eat his flesh and drink his blood have eternal life.[3] This Eucharistic Prayer traditionally mentions the vessel, so it is retained in the words of consecration.

The revised English translation changed the word from "cup" to "chalice." Jesus, of course, used a cup of some sort at the Last Supper, but the liturgical vessel has come to be known as a chalice. The word "chalice" evolved from the Latin word "calix," which appears in the Vulgate and the liturgical history of this prayer. Such cognates appear in the vernacular translations of other major language groups.

The revised English translation also changed the word "everlasting" to "eternal." The

> The Institution narrative of the Eucharistic Prayer is not meant to be a direct rendering of the biblical evidence, but to faithfully hand on the tradition.

word "everlasting" resembles the word "long-lasting" and implies measurable time, whereas "eternal" describes a mystery outside of time.

The word "shed" was changed to "poured out." The verb refers to the blood of Jesus flowing from his wounded body, as well as the blood contained in the chalice. A body sheds blood, but a chalice does not. The words "poured out" work for both images.

When the revised English translation appeared, the words for the Latin expression *"pro multis"* changed. Previously, the priest said Jesus shed his blood "for all," but now he says the more literal phrase, "for many." There is ample evidence that Jesus died for all,[4] but in Matthew's and Mark's accounts of the Last Supper, Jesus said he was pouring out his blood for many. He is surely alluding to Isaiah 53:12, which says God's servant will take away the sins of many. The text has more to do with Jesus' fulfillment of that prophecy than about any restriction of those who are saved.

---

2 Barba, p. 557.
3 See John 6:54.

4 See John 11:52; 2 Corinthians 5:14-15; Titus 2:11; and 1 John 2:2.

Questions for Discussion and Reflection

1. How well do the people hear the words of consecration over the wine? How does the priest make the gestures of showing the chalice and genuflecting?

_____

_____

_____

2. On what occasions does your community use incense at the consecration? Why then?

_____

_____

_____

3. The ringing of a bell is optional. Does your community exercise this option? Why or why not?

_____

_____

_____

4. When the priest shows the vessel, do the people look at it?

_____

_____

_____

---

91.   Then he says:

The mystery of faith.

And the people continue, acclaiming:

We proclaim your Death, O Lord,
and profess your Resurrection
until you come again.

Or:

When we eat this Bread and drink this Cup,
we proclaim your Death, O Lord,
until you come again.

Or:

Save us, Savior of the world,
for by your Cross and Resurrection
you have set us free.

After the Consecration when the Priest has said, *The mystery of faith*, the people pronounce the acclamation, using one of the prescribed formulas . . .

—GIRM, 151

See also GIRM, 37a.

Background

The priest announces the time for the Memorial Acclamation with the formula, "The mystery of faith." These elements are new to the 1970 Missal.

The First Letter to Timothy encourages deacons to hold fast to the mystery of the faith.[1] Possibly because of the way the deacon's liturgical ministry became linked to the administration of Holy Communion from the chalice, the words "the mystery of faith" began appearing

---

1   See 1 Timothy 3:9.

as a gloss in the words for the consecration of the wine by the seventh century.[2] They entered *The Roman Missal* in 1474.

In preparing the 1970 Missal, Study Group 10 proposed eliminating the text from the consecration of the wine for the sake of clarity.[3] At the same time, the members proposed adding a congregational acclamation into the Eucharistic Prayers at this point.[4] A text, which ultimately became the first of three options, was proposed in 1967.[5] It was designed for the three new Eucharistic Prayers, not for the Roman Canon, in imitation of Eastern Rite liturgies, and to enhance the active participation of the people. Furthermore, the text was proposed to be given "in these or similar words approved by the regional authority." A second such acclamation was envisioned for the last half of Eucharistic Prayer IV.[6]

In 1968 Pope Paul VI suggested moving—not removing—the words "the mystery of faith" from the consecration of the wine to the Memorial Acclamation, and to include them even in the Roman Canon. There they formed an invitation to the acclamation of the people.[7] At the same time, the other two options for this acclamation entered the preparatory work for the 1970 Missal.[8] The first acclamation is lifted from the venerable Antiochene Anaphora of Saint James, the Brother of the Lord.[9] The second

comes from Saint Paul.[10] The third is inspired by concepts in two other New Testament texts;[11] it is the only one that does not mention the second coming of Christ.

In one sense the acclamation does not harmonize well with the texts that follow. It was an afterthought to the composition of the Eucharistic Prayers, and the next section repeats its sentiments. The difference is that the people

> A proclamation is about someone or something, but an acclamation is directly addressed to someone. The people acclaim Christ; that is, they address their words to him.

make this acclamation to Jesus Christ, whereas the priest echoes the theme when rejoining his prayer to the Father. The design of the acclamation has the people responding to the invitation of the priest; he is not to make the acclamation himself, any more than he responds to other dialogues he initiates. This rubric became clearer in the revised English translation. The first one had the priest invite the response of the people with the words "Let us proclaim the mystery of faith." But this caused him to shift his focus from addressing the Father to addressing the people, and then joining them in addressing Christ, before returning his focus to the Father. Now it is clearer that his focus remains unchanged.

There is also a clearer distinction between the words "proclaim" and "acclaim." A proclamation is about someone or something, but an acclamation is directly addressed to someone. The people acclaim Christ; that is, they address their words to him. But here their words to him say that they are also proclaiming something about him, his death and Resurrection, the mystery of their faith.

---

2   Oury, p. 104.
3   Barba, p. 557.
4   Barba, pp. 424 and 426.
5   Barba, p. 520.
6   Barba, p. 583.
7   Barba, p. 675.
8   Ibid.
9   Prex, p. 249.

---

10 See 1 Corinthians 11:26.
11 See Revelation 5:9 and 1 Peter 1:18. See Raffa, p. 698.

Questions for Discussion and Reflection

1. How well does the Memorial Acclamation work in your community?

_____

_____

_____

2. Who makes the acclamation? The priest and the people? Or just the people?

_____

_____

_____

3. Do the people know all three versions? Who starts the acclamation? How do they know which one to begin?

_____

_____

_____

4. Some communities vary the acclamations by season. How do you decide which one will be used?

_____

_____

_____

92.   Then the Priest, with hands extended, says:

Therefore, O Lord,
as we celebrate the memorial of the blessed Passion,
the Resurrection from the dead,
and the glorious Ascension into heaven
of Christ, your Son, our Lord,
we, your servants and your holy people,
offer to your glorious majesty
from the gifts that you have given us,
this pure victim,
this holy victim,
this spotless victim,
the holy Bread of eternal life
and the Chalice of everlasting salvation.

. . . for as in these [prayers] the Priest enacts the anamnesis, while turned towards God likewise in the name of all the people, he renders thanks and offers the living and holy sacrifice, that is, the Church's oblation and the sacrificial victim by whose death God himself willed to reconcile us to himself . . . .

—GIRM, 2

See also GIRM, 4, 16, and 79f.

Background

This section ("*Unde et memores*") commemorates the Paschal Mystery (though no mention is made of the Second Coming of Christ) and offers to God the Bread of life and the Chalice of salvation. These words account for the anamnesis (remembering) and the offering of the sacrifice of the Mass. The practice of putting a commemoration after the Institution narrative was widely observed in ancient anaphoras.[1] Here the verbs are linked, "as we celebrate. . ., [we] offer." The previous English translation made the two actions equal: "recall . . . and . . . offer." But the revised translation properly makes the act of recalling subordinate to the act of offering. "Offer" stands alone as the main verb. The whole action remembers; this prayer concerns the offering.[2] The same relation

1   Cabié, *The Church at Prayer*, 2:97.
2   Mazza, p. 77.

between the verbs appeared in Ambrose's prayer, but enhancements have been made over the centuries.

God is addressed as "majesty," a word probably not inspired by the imperial court because it is found in the scriptures.[3] Ambrose used poetic language to describe the Body and Blood of Christ: "holy bread" and "the chalice of eternal life." These became amplified by the 1474 Missal.

That Missal and its successors called for a series of five Signs of the Cross over the elements. These have been eliminated in the 1970 Missal, partly for the principle of simplification, and partly because it appeared that the priest was blessing elements that had already been consecrated.[4] All in all, a clear distinction separates this section and the Preparation of the Gifts, which up to this time had been called the "Offertory."[5]

The victim is "pure," "holy," and "spotless." These attributes should also describe the Church making the offering. The whole action of offering will especially find favor with God if those who offer it are as worthy as the sacrificial elements.[6]

---

3 See, for example, Deuteronomy 5:24.

4 Barba, p. 362.

5 Barba, p. 274.

6 Mazza, pp. 78–79.

Questions for Discussion and Reflection

1. Especially with these words, the whole community offers itself to God together with the elements of sacrifice. How does the word "offer" stand out in this section of the prayer?

_____

_____

_____

2. Signs of the Cross have been eliminated from this section. Does this help focus on the meaning of the text on the offering?

_____

_____

_____

93.   Be pleased to look upon these offerings
with a serene and kindly countenance,
and to accept them,
as once you were pleased to accept
the gifts of your servant Abel the just,
the sacrifice of Abraham, our father in faith,
and the offering of your high priest Melchizedek,
a holy sacrifice, a spotless victim.

> . . . and the Priest also prays that the Body and Blood of Christ may be a sacrifice acceptable to the Father and which brings salvation to the whole world.
>
> —GIRM, 2

Background

This section ("*Supra quae*") asks God to accept these gifts in the tradition of those of Abel, Abraham, and Melchizedek. Of course, Christ is always acceptable to the Father. The prayer holds up the example of three Old Testament figures who found favor with God, in hopes that the praying community will as well.[1]

Although the Book of Genesis contains the stories of all three figures, they resurface in New Testament commentary. Abel is called "the just" in this prayer, a descriptor Jesus applied to him.[2] Paul calls Abraham the father of all believers.[3] Melchizedek is a type of Jesus.[4]

According to the *Liber pontificalis*, Leo the Great (+461) added the final modifiers, "a holy sacrifice, a spotless victim."[5] The words appear to describe the sacrifice of Melchizedek; Leo rebutted the Manichees who denied the holiness of all matter and hence of material sacrifice.[6]

This section is part of the core of the canon found in Ambrose, but there it appears after the section that now follows this one.

In the history of anaphoras, an epiclesis usually follows the anamnesis and offering, but there is no explicit calling upon the Holy Spirit in this section.

---

1   Miller, p. 281; Mazza, p. 80.
2   See Matthew 23:35; Genesis 4:4.
3   See Romans 4:11; Genesis 15:7–21; 22:1–14.
4   See Hebrews 7:3; Genesis 14:18–20.

---

5   LP 1:239; translation PT.
6   Fortiscue, p. 350.

Questions for Discussion and Reflection

1. This section of the prayer holds up the example of Abel, Abraham, and Melchizedek as models for the community's offering. How might your community fit the pattern of these Old Testament figures? What about you finds favor with God as you offer this sacrifice?

_____

_____

_____

94. Bowing, with hands joined, he continues:

In humble prayer we ask you, almighty God:
command that these gifts be borne
by the hands of your holy Angel
to your altar on high
in the sight of your divine majesty,
so that all of us, who through this participation
    at the altar
receive the most holy Body and Blood of your Son,

    He stands upright again and signs himself with the Sign of the Cross, saying:

may be filled with every grace and heavenly blessing.

    He joins his hands.

(Through Christ our Lord. Amen.)

It is, therefore, of the greatest importance that the celebration of the Mass or the Lord's Supper be so ordered that the sacred ministers and the faithful taking part in it, according to the state proper to each, may draw from it more abundantly those fruits, to obtain which, Christ the Lord instituted the Eucharistic Sacrifice of his Body and Blood and entrusted it as the memorial of his Passion and Resurrection to the Church, his beloved Bride.

—GIRM, 17

See also GIRM, 275b, and 368.

Background

This section ("*Supplices te rogamus*") asks for a holy angel to carry the gifts to God's altar in heaven, so that the earthly participants in the sacrifice may receive grace and blessing.

Ambrose's prayer has a similar section, though it calls upon "angels" in the plural, and the request precedes and blends with the reference to the sacrifices of Abel, Abraham, and Melchizedek. When the lines were reversed, the phrase "through this participation at the altar" was added to link the thoughts of the two sections. The "altar" is the one on high in both lines where it is mentioned. The community in the church on earth is mystically gathered at God's altar on high. The first English translation distanced the two altars, but they are one.

Many interpretations have been offered to identify the angel. Some have proposed that the angel is Jesus, or even the Holy Spirit, thus supplying a missing epicletic element. But the most logical conclusion is that the angel is just that— an angel. The prayer asks for the intervention of an intermediary to carry the gifts to God's altar.

It may be inspired by the biblical angel who stands at the altar with a golden censer, and who offers the prayers of the saints with the smoke of the incense.[1] Just as the Sanctus joins the voices of the earthly and the heavenly Church, so this prayer joins the offering of the Church to the action of an angel.[2]

The priest says this prayer while making a profound bow and signs himself with the cross as he stands upright again. This simplified the practice in the 1570 Missal, in which the priest bowed, placed his folded hands on the altar, kissed the altar, signed the host and the chalice with the cross, and then signed himself with the cross.

Another doxology concludes this section. This sets it apart from the intercessions for the dead that follow. For the 1970 Missal the words changed from "through the same Christ our Lord" to "through Christ our Lord," and they were made optional. The prayer that Ambrose recorded ends here.

1 See Revelation 8:3–4.
2 Mazza, pp. 81–83.

Questions for Discussion and Reflection

1. The priest bows low for this prayer and signs himself with the cross as he straightens up. How clear are these actions?

_____

_____

_____

2. How is the profound bow distinguished from other bows in the liturgy?

_____

_____

_____

95.　Commemoration of the Dead

With hands extended, the Priest says:

Remember also, Lord, your servants N. and N.,
who have gone before us with the sign of faith
and rest in the sleep of peace.

He joins his hands and prays briefly for those who have died and for whom he intends to pray.

Then, with hands extended, he continues:

Grant them, O Lord, we pray,
and all who sleep in Christ,
a place of refreshment, light and peace.

He joins his hands.

(Through Christ our Lord. Amen.)

. . . For the same reason [the Priest] should choose Masses for the Dead in moderation, for every Mass is offered for both the living and the dead, and there is a commemoration of the dead in the Eucharistic Prayer. . . .

—GIRM, 355c

See also GIRM, 79g.

Background

This section (*Memento etiam*) prays for Christians who have died, and allows the mention of some of their names. It parallels the section for the living that appears earlier in the canon. The prayer for the dead is not part of the earliest known version of the Roman Canon, nor is it recorded in the *Gelasian Sacramentary*. Alcuin included it, and it may have originated as a diaconal text in the eighth-century *Sacramentary of Padua*.[1]

The transition from the previous section is a bit abrupt. Not all celebrations of the Eucharist in the early Church included a prayer for the dead. Now it is a regular component. Prayer for the dead did not appear earlier in the anaphora because of the way the prayer for the living developed; it was added here before the anaphora draws to its close. The word "also" is probably intended to link this intercession all the way back to the one for the living. The appearance of prayer for the dead here provides a balance between parts of the anaphora, but it divides the intercessions, making the inner logic hard to follow.

---

1 Botte and Mohrmann, p. 24.

As with the prayer for the living, the faithful dead are called "servants." They have died "with the sign of faith," surely a reference to their Baptism. They now rest in the "sleep of peace" reserved for those who live in faith. The prayer asks God to grant all the faithful dead a place of refreshment, light, and peace. This intercession does not include nonbelievers; they were probably remembered in the Prayer of the Faithful during the early development of the Roman Canon.

Study Group 10 considered moving the intercession for the living to this point of the prayer, in order to achieve a more logical sequence. However it was decided not to tamper so dramatically with the long tradition of the Roman Canon.

This section closes with an optional doxology, drawing to a close the intercessions for the dead, a self-contained unit within the entire prayer. The only changes in the 1970 Missal were to reduce "through the same Christ our Lord" to "through Christ our Lord," and to make the entire phrase optional.

Questions for Discussion and Reflection

1. How does your community pray for the dead? Are they included in the Prayer of the Faithful?

_____

_____

_____

2. Do you ever hear the names of specific people in this part of the prayer? When? Why are they mentioned?

_____

_____

_____

96.   He strikes his breast with his right hand, saying:

To us, also, your servants, who, though sinners,

And, with hands extended, he continues:

hope in your abundant mercies,
graciously grant some share
and fellowship with your holy Apostles and Martyrs:
with John the Baptist, Stephen,
Matthias, Barnabas,
(Ignatius, Alexander,
Marcellinus, Peter,
Felicity, Perpetua,
Agatha, Lucy,
Agnes, Cecilia, Anastasia)
and all your Saints;

The *intercessions*, by which expression is given to the fact that the Eucharist is celebrated in communion with the whole Church, of both heaven and of earth, and that the oblation is made for her and for all her members, living and dead, who are called to participate in the redemption and salvation purchased by the Body and Blood of Christ.

—GIRM, 79g

See also GIRM, 318.

admit us, we beseech you,
into their company,
not weighing our merits,
but granting us your pardon,

He joins his hands.

through Christ our Lord.

Background

The intercessions conclude ("*Nobis quoque peccatoribus*") with another one for those present making this offering. Having prayed for the faithful dead, the worshippers now ask that they be numbered among them and the saints, many of whom are listed by name. These saints appear as sharers in God's company, not explicitly as intercessors. The "sinful servants" may refer either to the entire assembly of the faithful, or to the clergy.[1] The priest, speaking at least for himself, strikes his breast.

This section is not part of the earliest evidence of the canon, but it has parallels in many other early anaphoras.[2] It does appear in the 1474 Missal.

John leads the list of saints. In Latin, only his name is given—not his occupation; in theory

> John leads the list of saints. In Latin, only his name is given—not his occupation; in theory this could be any Saint John. However, the apostle was included in the first list of saints, so this has to be John the Baptist.

this could be any Saint John. However, the apostle was included in the first list of saints, so this has to be John the Baptist. For clarity, English-speakers retain the custom of using his full title. He parallels Mary, who stands at the head of the first list.

More biblical saints follow. Stephen the deacon and protomartyr comes next, and then Matthias and Barnabas, both of whom are called apostles in the New Testament, though they were not members of the original Twelve.

In the next group are Roman martyrs listed in chronological order: Ignatius of Antioch, Pope Alexander, Marcellinus the priest, and

Peter the exorcist, both of whom are remembered at the same titular church in the city of Rome.

Women martyrs follow this group of men. After Mary, these are the first women to be included among the many saints of the Roman Canon. They were probably added some years after the men, an early nod to the gender-equal witness of those who gloriously gave their lives for the faith. Felicity, Agnes, and Cecilia were early Roman martyrs over whose remains churches were built, and whose deaths were remembered with annual observances. Agatha and Lucy were Sicilian martyrs whose cult eventually extended to Rome. Anastasia was martyred in Sirmium in the East, but also earned a Roman following. Perpetua is most likely the martyr from North Africa who suffered together with her slave Felicity. As African martyrs, the two were always remembered as "Perpetua and Felicity," the slave mentioned last. However, the transposition of their names in the Roman Canon suggests that the Roman Felicity, already listed among the saints, was confused with the African Felicity, and Perpetua was added to accompany her memory. Hence, the list probably began as a group of Roman martyrs, but was populated with other women.[3] The net result is the listing of seven men (after John the Baptist) and seven women, as twelve apostles and martyrs were listed earlier in the prayer (after Mary).

By the Middle Ages, when Latin was less known and the clericalism of the Roman Rite was more cherished, priests recited the canon in a low voice. Amalarius requested that this section of the prayer, though, be offered aloud,[4]

---

1 Mazza, pp. 84–85.
2 Mazza, p. 85.

3 Jungmann 2:254.
4 Amalarius, *De ecclesiasticis officiis libri quatuor*, PL 105:1143.

because he thought it pertained to the conversion of all present, though the priest alone struck his breast. The instruction to proclaim this section aloud appeared in *The Roman Missal* from 1474 on.

The *Nobis quoque peccatoribus* traditionally concludes with a doxology, but not with an Amen, probably because the Amen that concludes the entire prayer follows shortly.

Study Group 10 considered abandoning this second list of saints, or at least shortening it.[5] It

also considered and rejected a proposal to move together the two prayers listing saints by name. With the restoration of the Prayer of the Faithful, it seemed that some of these intercessions would not be necessary.[6] Besides, the sentiments of this section seem to repeat those of the *Supplices*.[7] In the end, though, no major changes were introduced. The naming of most of has become optional, but when the option is taken, Mary remains the only woman mentioned by name in the Roman Canon.

---

6   Barba, p. 428.

7   Jungmann 2:248.

---

5   Barba, pp. 427, 451, 454.

Questions for Discussion and Reflection

1. On what occasions do you hear the entire list of saints in this section of the prayer? Why? What makes a good occasion for naming these saints?

_____

_____

_____

2. The priest strikes his breast at the beginning of this prayer. How well does this gesture convey the sincerity of his words, listing himself among the sinners of the Church?

_____

_____

_____

97.   And he continues:

Through whom
you continue to create all these good things, O Lord;
you sanctify them, fill them with life,
bless them, and bestow them upon us.

> For in [the Mass] is found the high point both of the action by which God sanctifies the world in Christ and of the worship that the human race offers to the Father, adoring him through Christ, the Son of God, in the Holy Spirit. . . .
>
> —GIRM, 16
>
> See also GIRM, 73.

Background

The body of the prayer concludes ("*Per quem haec omnia*") through Christ, through whom the Father continues to create and bless all things.

This section probably originated during a time when other gifts were presented for blessing, for example, the third to fourth centuries. *Apostolic Tradition* has prayers for blessing oil,

cheese, and olives after the Eucharistic Prayer.[1] This section may have been added as the priest regarded "all these good things" that God made through Christ.

The current practice omits a series of three signs of the cross over the host and the chalice. These accompanied the verbs of this section, but made it appear as though the priest were blessing elements that had already been consecrated.

---

1   AT 5 and 6.

Questions for Discussion and Reflection

1. The Roman Canon is a long prayer. As it reaches its conclusion, how well has its meaning been conveyed?

_____

_____

_____

2. Does the priest seem to understand the various parts?

_____

_____

_____

3. How well are the people able to join their minds and hearts with the priest?

_____

_____

_____

98. He takes the chalice and the paten with the host, and, raising both, he says:

Through him, and with him, and in him,
O God, almighty Father,
in the unity of the Holy Spirit,
all glory and honor is yours,
for ever and ever.

The people acclaim:

Amen.

Then follows the Communion Rite.

> The *concluding doxology*, by which the glorification of God is expressed and which is affirmed and concluded by the people's acclamation *Amen*.
>
> —GIRM, 79h

Background

The entire Eucharistic Prayer reaches its conclusion with a doxology. All honor and glory for ever and ever is offered to the Father; through, with and in Christ; in the unity of the Holy Spirit. The people's response is commonly called the great Amen. The rubrics never formally bestow on it that title, but that is the sense of this acclamation—a great Amen to a great prayer.

The practice can be traced all the way back to the second century. As Justin the martyr wrote, "When [the presider] has concluded the prayers and thanksgivings, all present give voice to an acclamation by saying: 'Amen.'"[1] Instructions to lift the consecrated elements can be found in *Ordo Romanus I*.[2]

The 1570 Missal instructed the priest to genuflect, make several signs of the crosses with the elements, and to lift them a little bit while he said or sang the doxology. In time, this became known as the "little elevation," because the elements had been lifted higher at the consecration. The text was said aloud and led directly into the

---

1   *First Apology* 65, cited in CCC, 1345.
2   OR I:89–90.

introduction to the Lord's Prayer. Contextually, it seemed more an introduction to the Communion Rite than the conclusion to the Eucharistic Prayer.

In 1964 Pope Paul VI ordered the priest to say the doxology aloud, to omit the signs of the crosses that had accompanied it, and to move the genuflection to a position after the Amen of the people.[3] The revised translation of the Missal says that the priest takes the chalice and the paten, "raising" them. The Latin word, *elevans,* suggests raising them higher than he does during the consecration, where he "shows" the elements to the people.

_____

3 Sacred Congregation of Rites (Consilium), Instruction *Inter oecumenici,* DOL 23:48f.

The current rite, in which the priest and people proclaim their respective parts of the entire prayer aloud, was able to make the Amen a more structural conclusion to the text. The doxology is assigned to the priest alone, the Amen to the people alone. In this way, the dialogue more naturally concludes the entire Eucharistic Prayer. In the United States of America, where the people kneel throughout the doxology, the change from the Eucharistic Prayer to the Lord's Prayer is made more evident also by their change in posture.

Questions for Discussion and Reflection

1. How well do the doxology and Amen serve as a conclusion to the Eucharistic Prayer in your community?

_____

_____

_____

2. The words are designed as a dialogue: the priest saying the doxology, and the people replying with an Amen. Are these roles respected?

_____

_____

_____

EUCHARISTIC PRAYER II

99. Although it is provided with its own Preface . . . , this Eucharistic Prayer may also be used with other Prefaces, especially those that present an overall view of the mystery of salvation, such as the Common Prefaces.

V. The Lord be with you.
R. And with your spirit.

V. Lift up your hearts.
R. We lift them up to the Lord.

V. Let us give thanks to the Lord our God.
R. It is right and just.

It is truly right and just, our duty and salvation,
always and everywhere to give you thanks, Father most holy,
through your beloved Son, Jesus Christ,
your Word through whom you made all things,
whom you sent as our Savior and Redeemer,
incarnate by the Holy Spirit and born of the Virgin.

Fulfilling your will and gaining for you a holy people,
he stretched out his hands as he endured his Passion,
so as to break the bonds of death and manifest the
    resurrection.

And so, with the Angels and all the Saints
we declare your glory,
as with one voice we acclaim:

Holy, Holy, Holy Lord God of hosts.
Heaven and earth are full of your glory.
Hosanna in the highest.
Blessed is he who comes in the name of the Lord.
Hosanna in the highest.

> Eucharistic Prayer II, on account of its particular features, is more appropriately used on weekdays or in special circumstances. Although it is provided with its own Preface, it may also be used with other Prefaces, especially those that sum up the mystery of salvation, for example, the Common Prefaces. When Mass is celebrated for a particular deceased person, the special formula given may be used at the proper point, namely, before the part *Remember also our brothers and sisters.*
>
> —GIRM, 365b
>
> See also GIRM, 79.

Background

That there is something called "Eucharistic Prayer II" is one of the most dramatic decisions of the Second Vatican Council. The long history of the Roman Rite maintained only one Eucharistic Prayer, the Roman Canon. Other Catholic and Orthodox Churches used more than one, and the expansion of repertoire in the Roman Rite happened partly because of their experience and influence on the Church's self-identity.[1] Although the Roman Canon is largely regarded as an invariable text, it employed a variety of alternative Prefaces, and it invited

---

1 Barba, p. 362.

seasonal changes within some of its sections. Pope John XXIII inserted Joseph into the list of saints. All these factors made it more possible to consider alternative anaphoras for the Roman Rite.

These were also possible because Eucharistic Prayer I was judged unsatisfactory for several reasons. It lacked an integrated theology of the Holy Spirit. The clarity of its original structure had been lost because of augmented sections. The list of the saints seemed at once too long and too restrictive. The participation of the people was minimal. Many of the priest's gestures seemed unnecessary and confusing. The text was difficult for people to follow because of its length and the lack of coherence and repetitious purpose among its sections. All these matters could be addressed with new Eucharistic Prayers.

The Church chose a lean design containing several parts: the thanksgiving, acclamation (Sanctus), the epiclesis, Institution narrative and Consecration, the anamnesis, the oblation, the intercessions, and the conluding doxology.[2] Most of these elements can be found in the Roman Canon, but not as cleanly as they would in the new prayers.

Study Group 10 expressed considerable interest in restoring some version of the Eucharistic Prayer from the third—fourth century-*Apostolic Tradition*,[3] regarding it as a model by which other Eucharistic Prayers could be added to the Roman tradition.[4] The prayer from the *Apostolic Tradition* appealed to the group because of its antiquity, simple structure, rich content, and use in Oriental Churches.[5]

Still, there were problems. The *Apostolic Tradition*'s prayer did not include a Sanctus or a section of intercessions. Some of its vocabulary needed updating to align with matters of faith. The study group also wanted to keep available the variety of Prefaces that gave the Roman Canon its flexibility. Members also discussed keeping within the new Eucharistic Prayers the same words for the Institution narrative and concluding doxology.[6] Gradually they developed a set of criteria for the new prayers, giving them a consistent structure.[7]

Eucharistic Prayer II was first proposed under the title of "Shorter Eucharistic Prayer."[8] Indeed, its brevity is still its most recognizable and popular feature. It is about one third the length of the Roman Canon.[9] As the text developed, it was considered a good option for Masses with children.[10]

This Eucharistic Prayer begins with the Preface Dialogue. So do the others, and a commentary on its parts appears above.[11] However, it is noteworthy that the earliest testimony for this dialogue is in the *Apostolic Tradition*. Because Eucharistic Prayer II is based on that ancient prayer, its opening dialogue is most faithful to the history of anaphoras.

The first line of the Preface did not originally appear in the *Apostolic Tradition*; it comes from a tradition starting at least in the *Veronese* and *Gelasian Sacramentaries*. In the interest of fluidity, it was added to make the transition between the dialogue and the body of the Preface.

The vocabulary of the Preface was corrected. For example, the *Apostolic Tradition* speaks of Jesus who, "conceived in the womb, was incarnate and manifested as your Son."[12] Today, this could be misconstrued to state that Jesus did not become incarnate until sometime after his conception, and was not manifested as the Son until after his birth. For consistency in Christology, the study group updated the words of this ancient Preface to say Jesus was "incarnate by the Holy Spirit and born of the Virgin."

As with the beginning of the Preface, its ending was added based on the style of other Prefaces in the Roman tradition. Furthermore, the entire Preface, though integral to the original anaphora, may be replaced by any alternate from others in today's Missal.

The Sanctus was not part of the prayer at the time of the *Apostolic Tradition*, but the study group added it here for the 1970 Missal. It interrupts the original logic of the text, but it makes the prayer more consistent with others in the developing Roman tradition.

---

2   See GIRM, 79.

3   Barba pp. 425, 475, 519.

4   Barba, p. 476.

5   Barba, p. 523.

6   Barba, p. 520.

7   Barba, pp. 579–580.

8   Barba, p. 521.

9   Barba, p. 585.

10 Barba, p. 524.

11 See p. 66.

12 AT 4:4.

Questions for Discussion and Reflection

1. Eucharistic Prayer II remains one of the most popular anaphoras in the Roman Rite. On what occasions does your community hear it?

_____

_____

_____

2. Do you hear a variety of Prefaces with this prayer? When do you hear the original one?

_____

_____

_____

3. On what occasions does your community sing the Preface Dialogue? The Sanctus?

_____

_____

_____

100.   The Priest, with hands extended, says:

You are indeed Holy, O Lord,
the fount of all holiness.

> . . . This people, though holy in its origin, nevertheless grows constantly in holiness by conscious, active, and fruitful participation in the mystery of the Eucharist.
>
> —GIRM, 5
>
> See also GIRM, 294.

Background

The prayer acknowledges God as the fount of all holiness. This line bridges the theme of the Sanctus, which declares God holy, and the epiclesis, which will call upon God to sanctify the bread and wine. God, who is holy, shares holiness.

This bridge did not appear in the *Apostolic Tradition*. It was unnecessary because there was no Sanctus. The study group drew the phrase "fount of all holiness" from the Mozarabic liturgy.[1] The post-Sanctus is very brief in Eucharistic Prayer II, especially when compared with Prayers I and IV.

---

1   Barba, p. 524.

Questions for Discussion and Reflection

1. This brief sentence plays an important structural role in the Eucharistic Prayer. How well is it appreciated by the priest and the people?

_____

_____

_____

2. In the United States of America the people are to kneel after the Sanctus. Does the presider wait for the community to settle down before starting these words? What affect does that have on the community's ability to pray?

_____

_____

_____

101. He joins his hands and, holding them extended over the offerings, says:

Make holy, therefore, these gifts, we pray,
by sending down your Spirit upon them like the dewfall,

> He joins his hands

> and makes the Sign of the Cross once over the bread and the chalice together, saying:

so that they may become for us
the Body ✚ and Blood of our Lord Jesus Christ.

> He joins his hands.

The *epiclesis*, in which, by means of particular invocations, the Church implores the power of the Holy Spirit that the gifts offered by human hands be consecrated, that is, become Christ's Body and Blood, and that the unblemished sacrificial Victim to be consumed in Communion may be for the salvation of those who will partake of it.

—GIRM, 79c

See GIRM, 9 and 78.

Background

The priest asks the Father to make the gifts holy by sending the Holy Spirit upon them. This epiclesis, with its explicit invocation for the coming of the Holy Spirit, is new to the history of the Roman Rite.

The study group preparing the text created this section because the epiclesis in the *Apostolic Tradition* came later—after the Institution narrative. The decision to include one shows the influence of the Eastern Rites over the development of the Roman Rite.

The image of the Holy Spirit coming like dewfall is taken from the seventh-eighth century *Gothic Missal*, where it appears in a Eucharistic Prayer for the Paschal Vigil.[1] Probably due to the difficulty of the image and the challenge of getting an appropriate translation, the first English translation of this prayer omitted the word "dewfall." In the Old Testament, God promises to be like dew for the sake of Israel, bringing forth new life.[2] Dew is a symbol of God's blessing descending.[3] A prophecy from Isaiah[4] inspired an Advent hymn, "Drop down dew," linking the image of dewfall to the coming of Christ, who brings salvation and justice to the morally parched earth.

While saying this text, the priest extends his hands over the offerings, and then makes the Sign of the Cross once over the bread and wine together. This constitutes a simplified gesture over the previous practice of making multiple signs of the cross over the elements, and a more unified theology by having the elements blessed together, not separately.

---

1 *Missale Gothicum, Rerum Ecclesiasticarum Documenta* (Rome: Casa Editrice Herder, 1961):271.

2 See Hosea 14:5–6.

3 See Psalm 133:3.

4 See Isaiah 45:8.

Questions for Discussion and Reflection

1. The priest's gestures accentuate the purpose of the text. How clear are the gestures?

_____

_____

_____

2. Many people assume that the priest has the power to change the bread and wine into the Body and Blood of Christ. What does this text say?

_____

_____

_____

102.　　In the formulas that follow, the words of the Lord should be pronounced clearly and distinctly, as the nature of these words requires.

At the time he was betrayed
and entered willingly into his Passion,

> He takes the bread
> and, holding it slightly raised above the altar, continues:

he took bread and, giving thanks, broke it,
and gave it to his disciples, saying:

> He bends slightly.

Take this, all of you, and eat of it,
For this is my Body,
Which will be given up for you.

> He shows the consecrated host to the people, places it again on the paten, and genuflects in adoration.

The *Institution narrative and Consecration,* by which, by means of the words and actions of Christ, that Sacrifice is effected which Christ himself instituted during the Last Supper, when he offered his Body and Blood under the species of bread and wine, gave them to the Apostles to eat and drink, and leaving with the latter the command to perpetuate this same mystery.

—GIRM, 79d

Background

The introduction to the Institution narrative says that Jesus entered his Passion willingly. He was not subject to the events around him; he chose to die for us. Part of his plan was leaving the memorial of his Passion, the Eucharist.

The *Apostolic Tradition* narrates the institution of the Eucharist, but more briefly than the words do now. The study group, having reworked this text for the Roman Canon, repeated it in the other Eucharistic Prayers.

For more on the words over the bread, see above.

103. After this, he continues:

In a similar way, when supper was ended,

He takes the chalice
and, holding it slightly raised above the altar, continues:

he took the chalice
and, once more giving thanks,
he gave it to his disciples, saying:

He bows slightly.

Take this, all of you, and drink from it,
For this is the chalice of my Blood,
The Blood of the new and eternal covenant,
Which will be poured out for you and for many
For the forgiveness of sins.

Do this in memory of me.

He shows the chalice to the people, places it on the corporal,
and genuflects in adoration.

. . . For Christ took the bread and the chalice, gave thanks, broke the bread and gave it to his disciples, saying: Take, eat and drink: this is my Body; this is the chalice of my Blood. Do this in memory of me. Hence, the Church has arranged the entire celebration of the Liturgy of the Eucharist in parts corresponding to precisely these words and actions of Christ, ...

—GIRM, 72

See also GIRM, 79.

Background

The introduction to the words over the chalice is briefer than those in Eucharistic Prayer I.

Gone are the nonbiblical descriptions of Jesus' hands and eyes. His words receive the focus.

For more on the words over the chalice, see page 82 above.

104. Then he says:

The mystery of faith.

And the people continue, acclaiming:

We proclaim your Death, O Lord,
and profess your Resurrection
until you come again.

Or:

When we eat this Bread and drink this Cup,
we proclaim your Death, O Lord,
until you come again.

Or:

Save us, Savior of the world,
for by your Cross and Resurrection
you have set us free.

Background

The Memorial Acclamation is the same in all
Eucharistic Prayers. See page 84 for comments.

105.   Then the Priest, with hands extended, says:

Therefore, as we celebrate
the memorial of his Death and Resurrection,
we offer you, Lord,
the Bread of life and the Chalice of salvation,
giving thanks that you have held us worthy
to be in your presence and minister to you.

Humbly we pray
that, partaking of the Body and Blood of Christ,
we may be gathered into one by the Holy Spirit.

Remember, Lord, your Church,
spread throughout the world,
and bring her to the fullness of charity,
together with N. our Pope and N. our Bishop*
and all the clergy.

In Masses for the Dead, the following may be added:

Remember your servant N.,
whom you have called (today)
from this world to yourself.
Grant that he (she) who was united with your Son in
          a death like his,
may also be one with him in his Resurrection.

The *oblation*, by which, in this very
memorial, the Church, in particular
that gathered here and now, offers the
unblemished sacrificial Victim in the
Holy Spirit to the Father. The Church's
intention, indeed, is that the faithful not
only offer this unblemished sacrificial
Victim but also learn to offer their very
selves, and so day by day to be brought,
through the mediation of Christ, into
unity with God and with each other,
so that God may at last be all in all.

—GIRM, 79f

* Mention may be made here of the Coadjutor Bishop, or Auxiliary Bishops, as noted in the *General Instruction of the Roman Missal*, no. 149.

Remember also our brothers and sisters
who have fallen asleep in the hope of the resurrection,
and all who have died in your mercy:
welcome them into the light of your face.
Have mercy on us all, we pray,
that with the Blessed Virgin Mary, Mother of God,
with the Blessed Apostles,
and all the Saints who have pleased you throughout the ages,
we may merit to be coheirs to eternal life,
and may praise and glorify you

He joins his hands.

through your Son, Jesus Christ.

Background

The prayer continues with a memorial of the death and Resurrection of Christ, in which the people offer the Bread of life and the Chalice of salvation. They pray for the Church, both the dead and the living.

Here the words "we offer you" signify the offering of the sacrifice to the Father. The words "bread" and "chalice" that appear in the *Apostolic Tradition* are amplified with scriptural modifiers ("of life"[1] and "of salvation"[2]) to express that the sacrifice is that which Jesus offered at the Last Supper.

The translation of the Latin word "*astare*" is rendered as "to be in your presence" instead of the more literal "to stand in your presence." In the United States of America the congregation kneels for this part of the Eucharistic Prayer.

A second epiclesis follows. In this case, the community prays that the Holy Spirit may gather into one those who partake of the Body and Blood of Christ. As the consecratory epiclesis is made over the bread and wine, so this prayer (albeit in the passive voice) invokes the Holy Spirit to come for the sake of unity. The wording that appears in Eucharistic Prayer II carries the force of this section from the *Apostolic Tradition*, but with clearer words. Both are inspired by a similar text in the *Didache*.[3] The study group added the Latin word "*Supplices*"

to the opening of this section,[4] probably to imitate a somewhat parallel section of Eucharistic Prayer I that begins the same way.[5]

Intercessions are made to bring the fullness of charity to the Church. This section was added to the text of the *Apostolic Tradition* because that anaphora did not have them. The study group sought to integrate this new section with the old. Originally, the new section put the references to the hierarchy and to the saints in the reverse positions. Thus, the second epiclesis bridged to the evocation of the saints, the dead were remembered, and then the prayer for the pilgrim Church and its hierarchy led to a concluding eschatological vision, followed by the doxology.[6] In the end, the order of these themes was altered, starting with prayers for the living Church and its hierarchy, moving to those for the dead, and then evoking the saints as the eschatological vision toward which the Church tends.

The intercessions resume with prayers for the dead. In Masses for the dead, the name of a specific person may be given. This section is usually included at funeral Masses, but may be used at any Mass for the dead. The request that the one who has died like Christ may rise like him is based on a letter of Paul.[7]

New to the Eucharistic Prayer of the Roman Rite is a petition for non-Christians. Intercession is made not only for those who have died "in

---

1 John 6:35, 48.
2 Psalm 116:13.
3 *Didache* 10:5.

4 Barba, p. 525.
5 OM 94.
6 Barba, p. 525.
7 See Romans 6:5.

the hope of resurrection" but also for "all who have died in your mercy."

The saints are named as those with whom the faithful wish to share eternal life. Their intercession is not requested as in the first listing of saints in Eucharistic Prayer I. Mary is the only saint mentioned by name; the apostles are here as a group. This wording is more ecumenically sensitive, allowing a broader range of Christians to join in the sentiments of Eucharistic Prayer II.

Questions for Discussion and Reflection

1. How does the priest's voice distinguish the sections of this prayer? Does he accent the words "we offer"?

_____

_____

_____

2. On what occasions do you use the special prayer for the dead?

_____

_____

_____

3. Does the reduced attention to the saints have its desired effect? This prayer does not offer the option of including the name of a specific saint. Why is it important to honor that?

_____

_____

_____

106. He takes the chalice and the paten with the host and raising both, he says:

Through him, and with him, and in him,
O God, almighty Father,
in the unity of the Holy Spirit,
all glory and honor is yours,
for ever and ever.

The people acclaim:

Amen.

Then follows the Communion Rite . . . .

Background

The doxology is the same as the one for Eucharistic Prayer I, but different from the one provided in the *Apostolic Tradition*: "through your Child Jesus Christ, through whom [be] glory and honor to you, Father and Son with the Holy Spirit, in your holy church, both now and to the ages of ages. Amen."[1] Unique to this doxology

---

1   AT 4.

is the inclusion of the Church as the place where glory and honor arise. However, in adapting this anaphora, the study group decided to change its doxology to match the one in other Eucharistic Prayers, especially because the creation of inter- cessions for this prayer put the Church in the preceding section.[2]

For comments on the doxology and Amen, see page 94.

---

2   Barba, pp. 525, 584.

EUCHARISTIC PRAYER III

107.   V. The Lord be with you.
       R. And with your spirit.

       V. Lift up your hearts.
       R. We lift them up to the Lord.

       V. Let us give thanks to the Lord our God.
       R. It is right and just.

Then follows the Preface to be used in accord with the rubrics, which concludes:

Holy, Holy, Holy Lord God of hosts.
Heaven and earth are full of your glory.
Hosanna in the highest.
Blessed is he who comes in the name of the Lord.
Hosanna in the highest.

Eucharistic Prayer III may be said with any Preface. Its use should be preferred on Sundays and festive days. If, however, this Eucharistic Prayer is used in Masses for the Dead, the special formula for a deceased person may be used, to be included at the proper place, namely after the words: *in your compassion, O merciful Father, gather to yourself all your children scattered throughout the earth.*

—GIRM, 365c

See also GIRM, 364.

Background

To fulfill the desire for newly composed anaphoras in the Roman Rite, Eucharistic Prayer III was created in imitation of the structure of Eucharistic Prayer II, while permitting the flexibility of preface usage preserved in Eucharistic Prayer I. This anaphora is not based on any previous text; it is inspired by old forms, while using contemporary images. By relying on the preface to articulate the reasons for giving thanks, the prayer was designed to be used at any season of the year.[1] It is about half the length of the Roman Canon.[2]

In preparing the text, the study group commissioned the composition of six different drafts.[3] Of these, the one that became Eucharistic Prayer III was the strongest, but still needed work.

For comments on the Preface Dialogue, see page 64. For the Sanctus, see page 69.

---

1   Barba, p. 549.
2   Barba, p. 585.
3   Barba, p. 519.

Questions for Discussion and Reflection

1. On what occasions does your community hear Eucharistic Prayer III?

_____

_____

_____

2. How often is the Preface Dialogue sung? The Sanctus?

_____

_____

_____

3. Do you hear the wide range of Prefaces offered by the Missal?

_____

_____

_____

108. The Priest, with hands extended, says:

You are indeed Holy, O Lord,
and all you have created
rightly gives you praise,
for through your Son our Lord Jesus Christ,
by the power and working of the Holy Spirit,
you give life to all things and make them holy,
and you never cease to gather a people to yourself,
so that from the rising of the sun to its setting
a pure sacrifice may be offered to your name.

> . . . The Eucharistic Prayer requires that everybody listens to it with reverence and in silence.
>
> —GIRM, 78
>
> See also GIRM, 79a.

Background

As the prayer unfolds, the people acknowledge their responsibility to praise God who created them.

A bridge to the Sanctus appears in the first line of the text, which calls God "indeed Holy." Because this prayer relies on the Preface to name the reasons for giving thanks, the post-Sanctus simply mentions God's role as the creator who ever gathers people to himself. These people rightly give God "praise"—a word introduced here in congruence with the new perception of the purpose of an anaphora: it is a Eucharistic Prayer, a prayer of praise and thanksgiving.

This section prepares for the epiclesis in two ways. It acknowledges that God who gives life to all things also makes them holy. Also, it mentions the Holy Spirit, in anticipation of the invocation that will follow.

The sacrificial nature of the Mass is affirmed with a reference to its Old Testament roots.[1] God spoke through Malachi that all nations from the rising to the setting of the sun would offer a "pure sacrifice." This Eucharist is set within that context.

---

1   See Malachi 1:11.

Questions for Discussion and Reflection

1. The third Eucharistic Prayer helps worshippers find their place and responsibility within creation. How does your community give thanks to God in the midst of the neighborhood where it gathers for prayer?

_____

_____

_____

2. You join churches around the world to offer a pure sacrifice to God. How does your community express its relationship to the universal Church? To the needs of the world?

_____

_____

_____

3. How well does the presider articulate the themes of holiness, praise, Spirit, and sacrifice?

_____

_____

_____

109.　He joins his hands and, holding them extended over the offerings, says:

Therefore, O Lord, we humbly implore you:
by the same Spirit graciously make holy
these gifts we have brought to you for consecration,

> He joins his hands
> and makes the Sign of the Cross once over the bread and
chalice together, saying:

that they may become the Body and ✚ Blood
of your Son our Lord Jesus Christ,

> He joins his hands.

at whose command we celebrate these mysteries.

The *epiclesis*, in which, by means of particular invocations, the Church implores the power of the Holy Spirit that the gifts offered by human hands be consecrated, that is, become Christ's Body and Blood, and that the unblemished sacrificial Victim to be consumed in Communion may be for the salvation of those who will partake of it.

—GIRM, 79c

See also GIRM, 179.

Background

The community implores the Lord to make the gifts holy by the Holy Spirit. The priest holds his hands extended over the offerings and makes one Sign of the Cross over them.

This section is based on the *Quam oblationem* from Eucharistic Prayer I,[1] the venerable section that began the Roman Canon in the writings of Ambrose. God is asked to make the gifts holy, so that they may become the Body and Blood of Jesus Christ.

The difference, of course, is that Eucharistic Prayer III makes an explicit reference to the Holy Spirit, and this was the intent of Study Group 10.[2] The Spirit had already been introduced in the previous section, so the transition to the epiclesis advances smoothly.

1　OM 88.

2　Barba, pp. 529 and 586.

This section asks God to make holy the gifts brought forth for consecration. It sounds a bit redundant, but the prayer is explicitly stating its ultimate request.

The gifts are those that "we have brought to you." This improves the previous English translation, which cast the line in the present tense: "we bring you these gifts." This section of the prayer was designed to look back to the Preparation of the Gifts. The gifts are not being brought forth now; they were brought forth earlier. The distinction is important because the revised Missal makes a strong case that the part of the Mass formerly called the "offertory" is not the offering; that will come during the Eucharistic Prayer. The gifts were brought at that time, and they will be offered to the Father after they are made holy by the Spirit.

The final line of this section, "at whose command we celebrate these mysteries," looks forward to the next section, the Institution narrative. The themes of the prayer are neatly interlaced from one section to the next.

Questions for Discussion and Reflection

1. The gestures of the priest are important for accompanying the meaning of the text. In your community, are they deliberate? Expressive?

_____

_____

_____

2. A deacon is instructed to kneel at this point. What does his posture demonstrate to the community?

_____

_____

_____

110.   In the formulas that follow, the words of the Lord should be pronounced clearly and distinctly, as the nature of these words requires.

For on the night he was betrayed

He takes the bread
and, holding it slightly raised above the altar, continues:

he himself took bread,
and giving you thanks he said the blessing,
broke the bread and gave it to his disciples, saying:

He bows slightly.

TAKE THIS, ALL OF YOU, AND EAT OF IT,
FOR THIS IS MY BODY,
WHICH WILL BE GIVEN UP FOR YOU.

He shows the consecrated host to the people, places it again on the paten, and genuflects in adoration.

The *Institution narrative and Consecration*, by which, by means of the words and actions of Christ, that Sacrifice is effected which Christ himself instituted during the Last Supper, when he offered his Body and Blood under the species of bread and wine, gave them to the Apostles to eat and drink, and leaving with the latter the command to perpetuate this same mystery.

—GIRM, 79d

See also GIRM, 78.

Background

The introduction to the Institution narrative is the shortest in all four of the Eucharistic Prayers in the Order of Mass. The line directly quotes Saint Paul's First Letter to the Corinthians: "[On the night he was betrayed."[1] From there, the story of the Last Supper continues as in the other Eucharistic Prayers. The word "For" subordinates this section to the previous one. As in Eucharistic Prayer I, this Institution narrative is not so much a reenactment of the Last Supper as a reason why the community praises God and asks for the coming of the Spirit.

For more comments on the consecration of the bread, see page 80.

---

1   See 1 Corinthians 11:23.

111.   After this, he continues:

In a similar way, when supper was ended,

He takes the chalice
and, holding it slightly raised above the altar, continues:

he took the chalice,
and giving you thanks he said the blessing,
and gave the chalice to his disciples, saying:

He bows slightly.

TAKE THIS, ALL OF YOU, AND DRINK FROM IT,
FOR THIS IS THE CHALICE OF MY BLOOD,
THE BLOOD OF THE NEW AND ETERNAL COVENANT,
WHICH WILL BE POURED OUT FOR YOU AND FOR MANY
FOR THE FORGIVENESS OF SINS.

DO THIS IN MEMORY OF ME.

He shows the chalice to the people, places it on the corporal, and genuflects in adoration.

Background

The introduction to the words over the chalice is similarly brief. They imitate those for Eucharistic Prayer II, though without the reference that this is happening "again," yet with two mentions of the chalice. The Latin mentions the chalice only once, but without a second mention in English, it may sound as though Jesus is giving the blessing to his disciples.

112.   Then he says:

The mystery of faith.

And the people continue, acclaiming:

We proclaim your Death, O Lord,
and profess your Resurrection
until you come again.

Or:

When we eat this Bread and drink this Cup,
we proclaim your Death, O Lord,
until you come again.

Or:

Save us, Savior of the world,
for by your Cross and Resurrection
you have set us free.

Background

For comments on the Memorial Acclamation,
see page 84.

113.   Then the Priest, with hands extended, says:

Therefore, O Lord, as we celebrate the memorial
of the saving Passion of your Son,
his wondrous Resurrection
and Ascension into heaven,
and as we look forward to his second coming,
we offer you in thanksgiving
this holy and living sacrifice.

Look, we pray, upon the oblation of your Church
and, recognizing the sacrificial Victim by whose death
you willed to reconcile us to yourself,
grant that we, who are nourished
by the Body and Blood of your Son
and filled with his Holy Spirit,
may become one body, one spirit in Christ.

In the celebration of Mass the faithful form a holy people, a people of God's own possession and a royal Priesthood, so that they may give thanks to God and offer the unblemished sacrificial Victim not only by means of the hands of the Priest but also together with him and so that they may learn to offer their very selves. They should, moreover, take care to show this by their deep religious sense and their charity toward brothers and sisters who participate with them in the same celebration. . . .

—GIRM, 95

See also GIRM, 79fg and 318.

May he make of us
an eternal offering to you,
so that we may obtain an inheritance with your elect,
especially with the most Blessed Virgin Mary, Mother of God,
with your blessed Apostles and glorious Martyrs
(with Saint N.: the Saint of the day or Patron Saint)
and with all the Saints,
on whose constant intercession in your presence
we rely for unfailing help.

May this Sacrifice of our reconciliation,
we pray, O Lord,
advance the peace and salvation of all the world.
Be pleased to confirm in faith and charity
your pilgrim Church on earth,
with your servant N. our Pope and N. our Bishop,*
the Order of Bishops, all the clergy,
and the entire people you have gained for your own.

Listen graciously to the prayers of this family,
whom you have summoned before you:
in your compassion, O merciful Father,
gather to yourself all your children
scattered throughout the world.

✚ To our departed brothers and sisters
and to all who were pleasing to you
at their passing from this life,
give kind admittance to your kingdom.
There we hope to enjoy for ever the fullness of your glory

    He joins his hands.

through Christ our Lord,
through whom you bestow on the world all that
    is good. ✚

* Mention may be made here of the Coadjutor Bishop, or Auxiliary Bishops, as noted in the *General Instruction of the Roman Missal,* no. 149.

Background

The people recall the death and Resurrection of Christ, and they look forward to his second coming. They offer the holy and living sacrifice to the Father. They ask to become one body, one spirit in Christ, filled with his Holy Spirit. Intercessions are made for the living and the dead.

This section opens with an anamnesis. Unlike the one in Eucharistic Prayers I and II, this one includes the second coming of Christ. As the community remembers the death, Resurrection and Ascension of Jesus, so it looks forward to his coming again. This section spells out the "mysteries" that the epiclesis in this prayer says the community celebrates.[1]

The offering takes place as the community celebrates this memorial. The "holy and living sacrifice" is offered. And it is done "in thanksgiving." This thanksgiving is the action of the community as it offers.

The following section, "Look, we pray," was much debated by Study Group 10.[2] The text

> The offering takes place as the community celebrates this memorial. The "holy and living sacrifice" is offered. And it is done "in thanksgiving." This thanksgiving is the action of the community as it offers.

is inspired by the Anaphora of Theodore of Mopsuestia: "We offer . . . this living and holy and acceptable sacrifice. . . by which you were appeased and reconciled, for the sins of the world."[3] But even this text derives from Paul's Letter to the Romans: "I appeal to you therefore, brothers and sisters, by the mercies of God, to present your bodies as a living sacrifice, holy and acceptable to God, which is your spiritual worship."[4]

The people ask God to look on the oblation of the Church and to recognize it as the Body and Blood of Christ. Specifically, the prayer says, "recognizing the sacrificial Victim." The Latin cognate one would expect, *Victima*, never appears in the Order of Mass. The word used

here is *hostia*, meaning "sacrifice." The word "Victim" has been criticized because it sounds as though the bloody sacrifice of Jesus is underway, which it is not.[5] But the word, which appeared in the former English translation, reappears in the revised.

The following line ("the Victim by whose death you willed to reconcile us to yourself") could be even more troubling. This revised English translation backs away from a literal rendering of this line, as the former also did. Literally, it says, "the Victim by whose death you willed to be pleased." It makes God sound bloodthirsty. The prayer simply intends to ask God to look upon the Church's offering, and see the offering of Christ, whose selflessness pleased the Father.

The community prays that those who are nourished by the Body and Blood of the Son and filled with his Spirit, may become one body, one spirit in Christ. This secondary epiclesis (as in Eucharistic Prayers II and IV, in the passive voice) implies that the Holy Spirit will fill the community in its communion, making the members one. As in Eucharistic Prayer II, this gift of the Holy Spirit is a gift of unity. The expression "one body, one spirit" can be found in the Anaphora of Basil.[6] But it also relies on the Letter to the Ephesians: "There is one body and one Spirit."[7] As the consecratory epiclesis asks for the gift of the Holy Spirit to change the bread and wine for the sake of communion, so this prayer assumes that the Holy Spirit through that communion will bind the participants in unity.

The intercessions for the Church open with another reference to the offering. In this case, the community asks that the Holy Spirit make them an "eternal offering" to the Father. That offering will open the gateway to sharing an inheritance with the saints.

The saints are mentioned here primarily as those whose company the community wishes to share, though the prayer acknowledges that the community relies on the saints' constant intercession. Mary is mentioned by name, the apostles and martyrs as a group. The saint of

---

1   OM, 109.

2   Barba, pp. 535–536, 545.

3   Anton Hänggi-Irmgard Pahl, *Prex eucharistica* Frieburg (Éditions Universitaires Fribourg Suisse, 1968):384, cited in Mazza, p. 322.

4   Romans 12:1.

5   Mazza, pp. 138–139.

6   Hänggi-Pahl 352, cited in Mazza, p. 323.

7   Ephesians 4:4.

the day or patron saint of the community may also be mentioned by name. This practice imitates the parallel section in the Roman Canon, but puts the list of saints in one place, shortens it considerably, and acknowledges the community's reliance on the intercession of the saints, without explicitly asking for it.

The next section prays for the peace and salvation of all the world. This kind of intention—extending beyond Catholic boundaries—was missing from Eucharistic Prayer I. The faithful pray that the sacrifice benefit not just themselves but everyone.

Then this section specifically prays for the Church—notably, the "pilgrim Church," an expression beloved by the Second Vatican Council.[8] The Pope and the local Bishop are prayed for by name; the order of Bishops, clergy, and the entire people are included. This condenses, restructures, and refocuses some of the material from the Roman Canon.[9]

The intercessions shift their focus to the needs of the worshipping community, here called "this family." Their prayer is to gather the children who are scattered. They do not specifically pray for themselves, but for those outside the fold, who are still called God's "children." Even the prayers for the dead remember both groups: "brothers and sisters" in the faith, and "all [outside the faith] who were pleasing to you at their passing from this life." Eucharistic Prayer III prays for the entire world, not just for the faithful.

To bridge this section and the concluding doxology, the community affirms that it hopes to enjoy the fullness of glory together with those who have died, through Jesus Christ.

---

8   See *Lumen Gentium*, 48, for example.

9   Eucharistic Prayer I; OM, 84 and 85.

Questions for Discussion and Reflection

1. How do you understand the expression "the sacrifice of the Mass"? How is sacrifice lived out in your community?

_____

_____

_____

2. Which saints are mentioned when your presider leads this section of Eucharistic Prayer III?

_____

_____

_____

3. This section sets a model of interceding for the needs of the Church and of all the world. How does your community live according to that model?

_____

_____

_____

114. He takes the chalice and the paten with the host and, raising both, he says:

Through him, and with him, and in him,
O God, almighty Father,
in the unity of the Holy Spirit,
all glory and honor is yours,
for ever and ever.

The people acclaim:

Amen.

Then follows the Communion Rite . . . .

Background

In composing a doxology for this new prayer, the one revised for the Roman Canon was adopted for the sake of uniformity.[1]

For comments on the doxology and Amen, see page 94.

---

1 Barba, p. 584.

115. When this Eucharistic Prayer is used in Masses for the Dead, the following may be said:

✚ Remember your servant N.
whom you have called (today)
from this world to yourself.
Grant that he (she) who was united with your Son in
    a death like his,
may also be one with him in his Resurrection,
when from the earth
he will raise up in the flesh those who have died,
and transform our lowly body
after the pattern of his own glorious body.
To our departed brothers and sisters, too,
and to all who were pleasing to you
at their passing from this life,
give kind admittance to your kingdom.
There we hope to enjoy for ever the fullness of your glory,
when you will wipe away every tear from our eyes.

. . . For the same reason he should choose Masses for the Dead in moderation, for every Mass is offered for both the living and the dead, and there is a commemoration of the dead in the Eucharistic Prayer. . . .

—GIRM, 355c

See also GIRM, 79.

For seeing you, our God, as you are,
we shall be like you for all the ages
and praise you without end,

He joins his hands.

through Christ our Lord,
through whom you bestow on the world all that is good. ✠

Background

During Masses for the dead—most commonly in funeral Masses—this section may replace the parallel shorter section in Eucharistic Prayer III.[1]

The community prays for a specific person by name. If this is a funeral Mass, or if the person has just died, the word "today" is inserted. The prayer requests that this faithful person, who died with Christ in Baptism, may rise with him in eternity. This echoes a line from Paul's Letter to the Romans.[2] The belief that God will "raise up in the flesh those who have died" is inspired by Job 19:26, and by the Christian belief in the Resurrection of the body. The belief that Christ will "transform our lowly body after the pattern of his own glorious body" comes from Philippians 3:21. The hope that they will enjoy God's glory "when you will wipe away every tear from our eyes" comes from Revelation 7:17 and 21:3–4. The belief that "seeing you, our God, as you are, we shall be like you" comes from 1 John 3:2. This section is more developed than the parallel section in Eucharistic Prayer II,[3] which clung to the spare language of the *Apostolic Tradition*. When Eucharistic Prayer III opens its voice to intercede for the dead, it speaks from a glorious collection of biblical sources.

1   OM, 113.
2   See Romans 6:5.

3   OM, 105.

Questions for Discussion and Reflection

1. When does your community use this section of Eucharistic Prayer III? Are there other opportunities for it?

_____

_____

_____

2. How do these images comfort those who have lost someone they loved? Those who are facing an imminent death?

_____

_____

_____

EUCHARISTIC PRAYER IV

116. It is not permissible to change the Preface of this Eucharistic Prayer because of the structure of the Prayer itself, which presents a summary of the history of salvation . . . .

> V. The Lord be with you.
> R. And with your spirit.
>
> V. Lift up your hearts.
> R. We lift them up to the Lord.
>
> V. Let us give thanks to the Lord our God.
> R. It is right and just.

It is truly right to give you thanks,
truly just to give you glory, Father most holy,
for you are the one God living and true,
existing before all ages and abiding for all eternity,
dwelling in unapproachable light;
yet you, who alone are good, the source of life,
have made all that is,
so that you might fill your creatures with blessings
and bring joy to many of them by the glory of your light.

And so, in your presence are countless hosts of Angels,
who serve you day and night
and, gazing upon the glory of your face,
glorify you without ceasing.

With them we, too, confess your name in exultation,
giving voice to every creature under heaven,
as we acclaim:

Holy, Holy, Holy Lord God of hosts.
Heaven and earth are full of your glory.
Hosanna in the highest.
Blessed is he who comes in the name of the Lord.
Hosanna in the highest.

Eucharistic Prayer IV has an invariable Preface and gives a fuller summary of salvation history. It may be used when a Mass has no Preface of its own and on Sundays in Ordinary Time. On account of its structure, no special formula for a deceased person may be inserted into this prayer.

—GIRM, 365d
See also GIRM, 78 and 79.

Background

In Eucharistic Prayer IV the Church has an anaphora styled within the Roman tradition, but inspired by Eastern sources, opening with a more complete treatment of the economy of salvation and including a consecratory epiclesis.[1]

For a while, Study Group 10 was advancing the use of the anaphora of Saint Basil in its entirety.[2] That prayer begins with thanksgiving for creation and continues with thanksgiving for salvation history up to the Incarnation. The words of institution use a formula synthesized from all the New Testament accounts. A consecratory epiclesis follows. A second epiclesis sanctifies the ones making the offering, and a great doxology concludes the prayer.

However, the congruence of this anaphora's theology required further examination, largely because of the location of its first epiclesis after the Institution narrative.[3] This raised practical questions, such as when the elevation should take place.[4] So even though the anaphora of Saint Basil was already in use by a wide variety of Eastern Churches,[5] it was not approved for inclusion in the 1970 Missal—by one vote.[6] Happily, Eucharistic Prayer IV, a new composition, preserved many of the features of the anaphora of St. Basil.

For comments on the opening dialogue, see page 64.

The first section of Eucharistic Prayer IV frequently addresses God as "Father most holy." The Latin is *Pater sancte,* without the superlative, but "Holy Father" is an English title for the Pope. The appearance of the title "Father" here probably derived from the first line of the Roman Canon.[7] Its uniqueness was lost in the previous English translation of the Mass, which frequently translated as "Father" the Latin word "Deus," meaning "God." Jesus used this expression "holy Father" when praying in John 17:11.

That God is "one" is affirmed in Deuteronomy 6:4. That God is "living" is attested by the apostle Peter in Matthew 16:16. That God is "true" is attested by Jesus in John 17:3.[8] That God dwells in unapproachable light is acclaimed in 1 Timothy 6:16, echoed in 1 John 1:5. Jesus states that God alone is good in Luke 18:19. God's role as the "source of life" is described in the first chapter of Genesis.

As the Preface recounts the creation of angels who serve and glorify God, it alludes to Jesus' saying that they continually see the face of the Father.[9] The community joins them in the song of all creation, the Sanctus.

For comments on the Sanctus, see page 69. However, it should be noted that the appearance of the Sanctus at this point in Eucharistic Prayer IV is one of its distinctive features. The text that follows forms a unit with what precedes. The Sanctus interrupts the flow when the prayer acknowledges the ministry of angels—because this is their song. It is thought that the Sanctus first entered its place within the anaphora exactly in a setting like this. Its usage gradually grew more widespread, even when the Preface did not explicitly deal with creation. In those cases, the theme of angels was inserted into the end of the Preface, so that the hymn would flow from it. But among the Eucharistic Prayers, the fourth preserves the most natural placement for singing the Sanctus.

Because of the integrity of the preface with the rest of the text, Eucharistic Prayer IV is not to be used when the Mass calls for a seasonal or festal Preface. It is intended for Ordinary Time.

> The first section of Eucharistic Prayer IV frequently addresses God as "Father most holy."

---

1 Barba, p. 587.
2 Barba, p. 519.
3 Barba, pp. 537–538.
4 Barba, p. 602.
5 Barba, p. 601.
6 Barba, p. 602.
7 OM, 84. See Mazza, p. 325.

8 Other citations abound. See Mazza p. 326.
9 See Matthew 18:10..

Questions for Discussion and Reflection

1. On what occasions does your community hear Eucharistic Prayer IV?

_____

_____

_____

2. Do you honor its Preface by not exchanging it with others?

_____

_____

_____

117.   The Priest, with hands extended, says:

We give you praise, Father most holy,
for you are great
and you have fashioned all your works
in wisdom and in love.
You formed man in your own image
and entrusted the whole world to his care,
so that in serving you alone, the Creator,
he might have dominion over all creatures.
And when through disobedience he had lost your friendship,
you did not abandon him to the domain of death.
For you came in mercy to the aid of all,
so that those who seek might find you.
Time and again you offered them covenants
and through the prophets
taught them to look forward to salvation.

And you so loved the world, Father most holy,
that in the fullness of time
you sent your Only Begotten Son to be our Savior.
Made incarnate by the Holy Spirit
and born of the Virgin Mary,
he shared our human nature
in all things but sin.
To the poor he proclaimed the good news of salvation,
to prisoners, freedom,
and to the sorrowful of heart, joy.

In the Eucharistic Prayer, thanks is given to God for the whole work of salvation, and the offerings become the Body and Blood of Christ.

—GIRM, 72b

See also GIRM, 5, 55, 57, and 357.

To accomplish your plan,
he gave himself up to death,
and, rising from the dead,
he destroyed death and restored life.

And that we might live no longer for ourselves
but for him who died and rose again for us,
he sent the Holy Spirit from you, Father,
as the first fruits for those who believe,
so that, bringing to perfection his work in the world,
he might sanctify creation to the full.

Background

After the Sanctus, the community gives thanks to God. The creation theme that appeared in the Preface expands into the salvation theme of the post-Sanctus. As a transition, this section acknowledges that God fashioned the world "in wisdom and in love."[1]

Humanity is the crowning point of God's creation. Genesis 1:27–28 says God created humans in his own image and entrusted the earth to their care.[2] The disobedience of the first humans is told in Genesis 3:6, and contextualized in salvation history in Romans 5:19. God's refusal to abandon those who sin is affirmed in Nehemiah 9:17. Humanity's anonymous search for God is described in Paul's sermon to Athenians worshipping an unknown God (Acts of the Apostles 17:27).[3] God's covenants with humanity were reestablished at various times in the scriptures; for example, with Adam, Noah, Abraham, Isaac, Jacob, and David.[4] The link between hope and salvation is stressed in Romans 8:24.

From creation, the prayer turns to the Incarnation and ministry of Jesus. It opens with references to John 3:16 (that God so loved the world to send the Son into it) and Galatians 4:4 (that the Son came in the fullness of time.) Jesus is given two titles: only-begotten Son, showing his relationship to the Father, and Savior, showing his relationship to the people he redeemed.[5]

Regarding the beginning of the life of Jesus, Luke 1:35 affirms that Jesus became incarnate by the Holy Spirit, and Mary asserts her virginity in the previous verse. In Eucharistic Prayer IV, this is the first of four times the Holy Spirit is mentioned. Hebrews 4:15 says Jesus became like us in all things but sin. All these passages inform this section of the prayer.

Jesus' ministry is summarized in his outreach to the poor, the prisoners, and the sorrowful of heart, in a reference to Luke 4:18, where

> Jesus' ministry is summarized in his outreach to the poor, the prisoners, and the sorrowful of heart

Jesus reads Isaiah 61:1 and applies the prophecy to himself. The death and Resurrection of Jesus is called God's "plan," a word that occurs in Ephesians 1:10 and 3:9. That Jesus "destroyed death and restored life" is stated in 2 Timothy 1:10.

After the Resurrection Jesus sent the Holy Spirit, who is mentioned a second time in the prayer, and the purpose of this sending relies on 2 Corinthians 5:15, "that we might live no longer for ourselves but for him." Jesus promises to send the Advocate in John 16:7. This Spirit is called the "first fruits" in Romans 8:23. The prayer understands the work of the Spirit as that of a sanctifier. Being holy, the Spirit makes others holy.

---

1   Proverbs 3:19; Psalms 136:5.
2   See also Psalm 8:6.
3   See Mazza, p. 166.
4   Mazza, p. 167.

5   Mazza, p. 167.

Questions for Discussion and Reflection

1. As you recall the great events of salvation history, does it feel as though the Eucharistic Prayer has mentioned the essential points?

_____

_____

_____

2. This section of the prayer relies on a widespread knowledge of sacred scripture. How can you help people appreciate the many scriptural references to redemption, creation, and the life and ministry of Jesus, who sends the Holy Spirit?

_____

_____

_____

118.   He joins his hands and, holding them extended over the offerings, says:

Therefore, O Lord, we pray:
may this same Holy Spirit
graciously sanctify these offerings,

> He joins his hands
> and makes the Sign of the Cross once over the bread and
chalice together, saying:

that they may become
the Body and ✛ Blood of our Lord Jesus Christ

> He joins his hands.

for the celebration of this great mystery,
which he himself left us
as an eternal covenant.

> Now the center and high point of the entire celebration begins, namely, the Eucharistic Prayer itself, that is, the prayer of thanksgiving and sanctification. . . .
>
> —GIRM, 78
>
> See also GIRM, 79c and 281.

Background

The epiclesis draws on the previous theme of the coming of the Holy Spirit for sanctification, and formally asks God to let the Holy Spirit sanctify the gifts of bread and wine. This is the third mention of the Holy Spirit, and it flows naturally from the work of the Spirit in salvation history.

This epiclesis resembles those that appear in Eucharistic Prayers II and III. The absence of such a petition in Eucharistic Prayer I was seen as a deficiency that the new prayers should address.

The form of address changes in this section of Eucharistic Prayer IV. Up to this time, it has addressed God as "Father most holy" or "Father." Now it turns to God as "Lord," acknowledging humbly the distance of the suppliants making the anaphora's principal request.

This epiclesis asks for the Spirit to "sanctify" these gifts, rather than consecrate them as

Eucharistic Prayer III implies.[1] The choice of "sanctify" unites this section to the work of the Spirit earlier in salvation history,[2] and with the sanctification of the people in the forthcoming second epiclesis. The language has had positive ecumenical significance and pastoral success.[3]

The transition to the Institution narrative happens through a reference to the "great mystery," the "eternal covenant," which came to light in the events at the Last Supper.

---

1 OM, 109.
2 See last sentence of OM, 117.

3 Mazza, pp. 170–171.

Questions for Discussion and Reflection

1. The priest extends his hands over the offerings and makes the Sign of the Cross over them. How deliberate are these actions? Do they adequately convey the sense of what is happening?

_____

_____

_____

2. This is one of the most significant moments of a Eucharistic Prayer. How well is this conveyed to the people?

_____

_____

_____

119.   In the formulas that follow, the words of the Lord should be pronounced clearly and distinctly, as the nature of these words requires.

For when the hour had come
for him to be glorified by you, Father most holy,
having loved his own who were in the world,
he loved them to the end:
and while they were at supper,

> He takes the bread
> and, holding it slightly raised above the altar, continues:

he took bread, blessed and broke it,
and gave it to his disciples, saying:

> He bows slightly.

TAKE THIS, ALL OF YOU, AND EAT OF IT,
FOR THIS IS MY BODY,
WHICH WILL BE GIVEN UP FOR YOU.

> He shows the consecrated host to the people, places it again on the paten, and genuflects in adoration.

So, in the new Missal the rule of prayer (lex orandi) of the Church corresponds to her perennial rule of faith (lex credendi), by which we are truly taught that the sacrifice of his Cross and its sacramental renewal in the Mass, which Christ the Lord instituted at the Last Supper and commanded his Apostles to do in his memory, are one and the same, differing only in the manner of their offering; and as a result, that the Mass is at one and the same time a sacrifice of praise, thanksgiving, propitiation and satisfaction.

—GIRM, 2

See also GIRM, 72, 79, and 83.

Background

The Institution narrative is essentially the same as the one that appears in the other Eucharistic Prayers. However, the introduction, faithful to the style of Eucharistic Prayer IV, relies on two passages from John's account of the Gospel. It recalls that the hour had come for Jesus to be glorified,[1] and that, "having loved his own who were in the world, he loved them to the end."[2]

As in the other new Eucharistic Prayers, the nonbiblical references to Jesus' eyes and

---

1   See John 17:1.
2   John 13:1.

hands in Eucharistic Prayer I were not retained. When describing the actions of Jesus, this Eucharistic Prayer says he "blessed and broke" the bread. In other prayers it says Jesus "said the blessing," to avoid the implication that Jesus blessed the bread. He blessed God. The Latin verb is identical in Eucharistic Prayers I, III and IV, but the English says "blessed" in Eucharistic Prayer IV. Ironically, the previous translation of this Eucharistic Prayer has "[Jesus] said the blessing." The blessing of objects came later in Church history; in the Bible, Jesus blessed (that is, praised) God.

For more comments on the words concerning the bread, see page 80.

120.   After this, he continues:

In a similar way,

He takes the chalice
and, holding it slightly raised above the altar, continues:

taking the chalice filled with the fruit of the vine,
he gave thanks,
and gave the chalice to his disciples, saying:

He bows slightly.

TAKE THIS, ALL OF YOU, AND DRINK FROM IT,
FOR THIS IS THE CHALICE OF MY BLOOD,
THE BLOOD OF THE NEW AND ETERNAL COVENANT,
WHICH WILL BE POURED OUT FOR YOU AND FOR MANY
FOR THE FORGIVENESS OF SINS.

DO THIS IN MEMORY OF ME.

He shows the chalice to the people, places it on the corporal, and genuflects in adoration.

Background

The Institution narrative continues with the words over the chalice. The expression "the fruit of the vine" alludes to Matthew 26:29, where Jesus says he will not drink it again until he drinks it with them new in the kingdom of his Father.

121.   Then he says:

The mystery of faith.

And the people continue, acclaiming:

We proclaim your Death, O Lord,
and profess your Resurrection
until you come again.

Or:

When we eat this Bread and drink this Cup,
we proclaim your Death, O Lord,
until you come again.

Or:

Save us, Savior of the world,
for by your Cross and Resurrection
you have set us free.

Background

For comments on the Memorial Acclamation,
see page 84.

122.   Then, with hands extended, the Priest says:

Therefore, O Lord,
as we now celebrate the memorial of our redemption,
we remember Christ's Death
and his descent to the realm of the dead,
we proclaim his Resurrection
and his Ascension to your right hand,
and, as we await his coming in glory,
we offer you his Body and Blood,
the sacrifice acceptable to you
which brings salvation to the whole world.

Look, O Lord, upon the Sacrifice
which you yourself have provided for your Church,
and grant in your loving kindness
to all who partake of this one Bread and one Chalice

In truth, the nature of the ministerial Priesthood proper to the Bishop and the Priest, who offer the Sacrifice in the person of Christ and who preside over the gathering of the holy people, shines forth in the form of the rite itself, on account of the more prominent place and function given to the Priest. . . .

—GIRM, 4

See also GIRM, 79.

that, gathered into one body by the Holy Spirit,
they may truly become a living sacrifice in Christ
to the praise of your glory.

Therefore, Lord, remember now
all for whom we offer this sacrifice:
especially your servant, N. our Pope,
N. our Bishop,* and the whole Order of Bishops,
all the clergy,
those who make this offering,
those gathered here before you,
your entire people,
and all who seek you with a sincere heart.

Remember also
those who have died in the peace of your Christ
and all the dead,
whose faith you alone have known.

To all of us, your children,
grant, O merciful Father,
that we may enter into a heavenly inheritance
with the Blessed Virgin Mary, Mother of God,
and with your Apostles and Saints in your kingdom.
There, with the whole of creation,
freed from the corruption of sin and death,
may we glorify you through Christ our Lord,

> He joins his hands.

through whom you bestow on the world all that is good.

---

* Mention may be made here of the Coadjutor Bishop, or Auxiliary Bishops, as noted in the *General Instruction of the Roman Missal*, no. 149.

Background

The anamnesis, offering, and intercessions conclude the main body of the Eucharistic Prayer.

As in other Eucharistic Prayers, the Institution narrative has led to the Memorial Acclamation, which in turn leads to the anamnesis and offering. The link is so strong that all the prayers begin this section with the word "Therefore."

Christ commanded his followers to do this in his memory, and "therefore" they do it.

The community is celebrating the memorial of the redemption, remembering the components of the Paschal Mystery: the death of Christ, his descent to the realm of the dead, his Resurrection, Ascension, and his future coming in glory. The anamnesis of this Eucharist Prayer is thorough, even including the second coming, as does Eucharistic Prayer III. It resembles the elements that anchor the middle part of the Creed.

The offering is placed squarely within the act of remembering. As the community remembers the Paschal Mystery, it makes its offering. Just as the people remember what Jesus did, and what command he gave, so they fulfill that command by doing what he died: offering. The specific offering is described in two ways: the "Body and Blood" of Christ and "the sacrifice."

The prayer relies on New Testament passages to describe this sacrifice. Ephesians 5:2 says Jesus gave himself as a fragrant offering and sacrifice to God. Hebrews 10:8–9 applies Psalm 40:6–8 to Christ; the Father is not pleased by the offerings of the old law, but by the sacrifice of the Son. It is a single offering[1], not one that is repeated. The supper is repeated, but not the mystery of redemption.[2]

The second epiclesis of Eucharistic Prayer IV asks that the Lord will look upon the sacrifice being offered and to make the community a living sacrifice in Christ. This is achieved through the action of the Holy Spirit, who gathers those who will share communion into one.

The opening image alludes to Genesis 22:8, where Abraham tells his son Isaac that God will provide a lamb for the offering. Here, the community asks the Lord to look upon the Sacrifice he has provided for the Church.

The prayer for the Church presumes that those present will be participating in the "one Bread and one Chalice," an allusion to 1 Corinthians 10:16–17, where Paul affirms the unity of those who share the one bread, the body of Christ.

This community is gathered into one as though its members had been scattered, or at least are away from their true home. A similar sentiment appears in the same epiclesis of Eucharistic Prayer II.[3] The historic backdrop for this image concerns Israel's years of exile. God, who had scattered them from their homeland, promised to bring them back—all of them, even the infirm. The theme of gathering the scattered appears in Jeremiah 31:8–10. In the New Testament, John's account of the Gospel frequently expresses the mission of Jesus in terms of a gathering unity. At the Last Supper, Jesus prayed for the unity of his followers so that others might believe through them.[4] Shortly before his arrest, he announced, "when I am lifted up from the earth, [I] will draw all people to myself."[5] John explains that the purpose of Jesus' death was "to gather into one the dispersed children of God" (11:52). Unity, then, is the fruit of Christ's death.[6] Those who participate in the mystery of his death through these sacramental signs are brought together in unity.

The Holy Spirit unites the people. Jesus promised to send the Spirit.[7] As the previous section remembered the death, Resurrection and Ascension of Jesus, so now the prayer of the Church relies upon the ascended Jesus to send the Spirit as he promised.[8] Utilizing the passive voice as in Eucharistic Prayers II and III, Eucharistic Prayer IV implies that the Spirit is responsible for gathering the community into one as its members partake of the one Bread and one Chalice.

This intercessory prayer aims to make the community a living sacrifice. Paul asks the Romans[9] to present themselves as a living sacrifice, holy and acceptable to God. Ephesians 1:12 says that those who set their hopes in Christ live for the praise of his glory. These passages have been linked to make the point of this intercession: that the community may "become a living sacrifice in Christ to the praise of your glory."

During its deliberations, Study Group 10 suggested that the people make another acclamation at this point in the prayer. Having completed the anamnesis, the offering and the second epiclesis, the people could appropriately make another intervention in the sweep of the prayer. The following text was suggested: "We praise you, we bless you, we glorify you. Be gracious, Lord, and have mercy on all."[10] It was not intended to be obligatory, and such acclamations were proposed "in these or similar words approved by the territorial authority."[11] However, this additional acclamation did not survive.

---

1   See Hebrews 10:14.
2   Mazza, p. 177.
3   OM, 105.
4   See John 17:21-23.
5   John 12:32.
6   Mazza, p. 184.
7   For example, John 14:16-17.
8   Mazza, pp. 180–182.
9   See Romans 12:1.
10   Barba, p. 599.
11   Barba, p. 583.

The intercessions for the living and the dead follow the second epiclesis. The opening word, "Therefore," shows that the next petitions flow from the previous one. As the community has prayed for unity, so now it requests more, asking the Lord to remember the living and the dead. The repeated word "remember" links these next two sections, and the opening phrase, "all for whom we make this offering," governs both parts.

The living are listed in hierarchical order. The Pope and the Bishop are listed by name, as is customary. All the bishops and all clergy are mentioned next. Then the prayer mentions "those who make the offering" and "those gathered here"—referring to the clergy and the faithful present at this celebration of the Eucharist. Then the "entire people" of God, which will include all the baptized not present. The expression, a favorite of the Second Vatican Council,[12] refers to the entire Church, not the least members of the hierarchy; it is drawn from 1 Peter 2:9, which calls the faithful "a chosen race, a royal priesthood, a holy nation, God's own people."

Included among the living are "all who seek you with a sincere heart." This includes non-Christians, a group ignored in Eucharistic Prayer I. The line probably alludes to Jeremiah 29:13–14, "When you search for me, you will find me; if you seek me with all your heart, I will let you find me." The line builds on the belief that Jesus died for the sake of all, as indicated in his own prediction that he would draw all to himself when he would be lifted up.[13] This part of Eucharistic Prayer IV should counterbalance a minimalistic interpretation of a line from the Institution narrative, that Jesus died for "many."[14]

The prayers for the dead also begin with a request that God "remember" them. They are called "those who have died in the peace of your Christ," probably an allusion to Colossians 3:15, where Paul asks that his readers may be ruled by the peace of Christ, in which they were called.

The community also prays for those "whose faith you alone have known." As Eucharistic Prayer IV explicitly prayed for living non-Christians, so it also prays for the deceased of indeterminable faith. The Good Shepherd says, "I know my own and my own know me."[15] 2 Timothy 2:19 says, "The Lord knows those who are his."

The prayer returns to addressing God with the title "Father," as the community asks that all may enter "a heavenly inheritance." 1 Peter 1:4 says that the faithful have received a new birth into an inheritance that is imperishable. Romans 8:17 says the faithful are joint heirs with Christ. Jesus told Simon Peter, "Unless I wash you, you have no share with me."[16]

Several saints are mentioned—Mary by name and with the titles "Virgin" and "Mother of God." The apostles and other saints are mentioned as a group. But all of them are simply mentioned as sharers of the inheritance in which all the children of God long to partake. Eucharistic Prayer IV does not directly call for the intercession of the saints.

These petitions conclude with a prayer that the community may be freed from the corruption of sin and death and glorify God through Christ, together with all of creation. As the prayer began with God's creation, so it ends with creation's praise of God. The language relies on Romans 8:21, where Paul says creation has hope that it "will be set free from its bondage to decay and will obtain the freedom of the glory of the children of God." A few verses later, he says, "those whom [God] predestined he also called, and those whom he called he also justified; and those whom he justified he also glorified."[17] Romans 6:18 also says the faithful have been set free from sin. The point returns a few verses later, where Paul says "the advantage you get is sanctification. The end is eternal life."[18]

Eucharistic Prayers II and III were composed with special commemorations for use during Masses of the Dead, but Eucharistic Prayer IV does not have one because of the integrity of its text. It was not designed for use at Masses of the Dead.

---

12 See *Lumen gentium*, chapter II.
13 See John 12:32.
14 See above.

15 John 10:14.
16 John 13:8.
17 Romans 8:30.
18 Romans 6:22.

Questions for Discussion and Reflection

1. The offering is made as the community remembers the death of Christ. In what ways does your worshipping community imitate the death and rising of Christ outside the liturgy?

_____

_____

_____

2. The second epiclesis relies on the unity of the Church to be a living sacrifice in Christ. What are good examples of the unity of your worshipping community?

_____

_____

_____

3. As you pray for the living and the dead, how clear is it that you intend to include nonbelievers as well? How does your community practice evangelization?

_____

_____

_____

123.   He takes the chalice and the paten with the host and, raising both, he says:

Through him, and with him, and in him,
O God, almighty Father,
in the unity of the Holy Spirit,
all glory and honor is yours,
for ever and ever.

The people acclaim:

Amen.

Then follows the Communion Rite . . . .

Background

No change was made to the doxology and Amen that conclude the Eucharistic Prayer. It was decided to keep these uniform throughout. For commentary, see page 94.

THE COMMUNION RITE

124. After the chalice and paten have been set down, the Priest, with hands joined, says:

At the Savior's command
and formed by divine teaching,
we dare to say:

He extends his hands and, together with the people, continues:

Our Father, who art in heaven,
hallowed be thy name;
thy kingdom come,
thy will be done
on earth as it is in heaven.
Give us this day our daily bread,
and forgive us our trespasses,
as we forgive those who trespass against us;
and lead us not into temptation,
but deliver us from evil.

> In the Lord's Prayer a petition is made for daily bread, which for Christians means principally the Eucharistic Bread, and entreating also purification from sin, so that what is holy may in truth be given to the holy. . . .
>
> —GIRM, 81
>
> See also GIRM, 36, 41, and 152.

Background

The Communion Rite of the Mass begins with the Lord's Prayer. As the faithful prepare to share Holy Communion, they offer the best prayer they know, the one that Jesus taught

> Matthew and Luke both record the Lord's Prayer, but Matthew's version enjoys popular usage.

his disciples. It probably ended up as a prayer before Holy Communion because of the petition for daily bread and its promotion of mutual forgiveness.

Matthew and Luke both record the Lord's Prayer, but Matthew's version enjoys popular usage.[1] Luke's is shorter,[2] and therefore may be closer to the original. It is more likely that Matthew expanded the verses than that Luke omitted some. But the full text of Matthew's version has been adopted for generations, starting with the *Didache*, around the turn of the second

century.[3] The *Didache* recommends praying the Lord's Prayer three times a day,[4] but there was no daily Mass at the time, and no clear indication that it was part of the Eucharist.

The earliest clear testimony of the Lord's Prayer in the context of the Communion Rite is in *Sacraments* by Ambrose (+397).[5] Gregory the Great says that he moved it to its present position immediately after the Roman Canon, in keeping with the practice in the East.[6] He also says that in Rome the priest recited it alone, whereas it was said among the Greeks by all the people together.[7]

That Roman custom endured through the use of the 1474 Missal up to the twentieth century. The priest recited the Lord's Prayer himself in a low voice, raising it for the final line of the prayer. In 1958, at spoken Masses, all were permitted to recite the Lord's Prayer together

---

1   See Matthew 6:9–13.
2   See Luke 11:2–4.

3   *Didache* 8:2.
4   *Didache* 8:3.
5   *De sacramentis* 5:20–30, SChr 25:94.
6   *Letter* 9:26, CCL 40A:586–587.
7   Ibid.

in Latin.[8] In 1964, Pope Paul VI permitted the entire congregation to sing it in Latin, and in the vernacular with the permission of the territorial ecclesiastical authority.[9] Even at this time, the priest added an "Amen" to the conclusion of the prayer, but this was omitted in the reformed liturgy,[10] probably because there is no Amen in Matthew's account of the Gospel. The Amen concluded the prayer for devotional purposes outside of Mass, and the priest immediately continued praying at the conclusion of the Our Father.

8   Sacra Rituum Congregatio, *Instructio "de musica sacra et sacra Liturgia"* (3 septembris 1958) n. 32, AAS 50 (1958) 643.

9   *Inter oecumenici* DOL 23:48g.

10 Barba, p. 292.

Questions for Discussion and Reflection

1. The Lord's Prayer immediately follows the Eucharistic Prayer. In the presence of the consecrated elements, no prayer of human composition takes precedence. How does your community make the distinction between the Eucharistic Prayer and the Lord's Prayer?

_____

_____

_____

2. The priest extends his hands for the prayer. How clear is the meaning of his gesture and the tone of his voice?

_____

_____

_____

3. On what occasions does your community sing the Lord's Prayer? How do you decide when?

_____

_____

_____

4. Does your community exercise other customs with regard to the Lord's Prayer? Which ones? Why?

_____

_____

_____

125. With hands extended, the Priest alone continues, saying:

Deliver us, Lord, we pray, from every evil,
graciously grant peace in our days,
that, by the help of your mercy,
we may be always free from sin
and safe from all distress,
as we await the blessed hope
and the coming of our Savior, Jesus Christ.

He joins his hands.

The people conclude the prayer, acclaiming:

For the kingdom,
the power and the glory are yours
now and for ever.

> . . . The embolism, developing the last petition of the Lord's Prayer itself, asks for deliverance from the power of evil for the whole community of the faithful.
>
> The invitation, the Prayer itself, the embolism, and the doxology by which the people conclude these things are sung or are said aloud.
>
> —GIRM, 81
>
> See also GIRM, 41 and 153.

Background

Following the Lord's Prayer, the priest prays that the community may be delivered from every evil as it awaits the coming of Jesus. Because it is an insertion, this prayer is called an embolism. *Ordo Romanus I* attests to the closing line of this prayer, indicating it was in use by the sixth or seventh century.[1]

The text handed down through the history of *The Roman Missal* have implored the intercession of Mary, Peter, Paul, and Andrew, and was said by the priest in a low voice while he signed

> The embolism closes with a doxology that is well known today among Protestant Christians, but that Catholics did not retain as the conclusion to the Lord's Prayer.

himself with the paten and then kissed it. In 1964 Pope Paul VI asked the priest to say the prayer out loud.[2] Study Group 10 eliminated the names of the saints[3] because of the length of the prayer that would now be recited aloud, and because the mention of the saints was a duplication of material in the Roman Canon.[4] The gestures of the priest were eliminated. The study group also expanded the conclusion with a direct reference to Titus 2:13, which equates our hope with the future coming of Jesus. The verse is part of the second reading for Christmas Midnight Mass. As the Memorial Acclamation enriched the Eucharistic Prayer with a reference to the future coming of Christ, so the embolism was amplified to serve the same purpose.[5]

The embolism closes with a doxology that is well known today among Protestant Christians, but that Catholics did not retain as the conclusion to the Lord's Prayer. It was probably added by early Christians to give the Our Father a resounding conclusion; it then appeared in some early manuscripts of Matthew's account of the Gospel and in the *Didache*. The custom of displacing the acclamation from the body of the Lord's Prayer came after the Second Vatican Council. Over a few objections, it was added to the Communion Rite partly because of its usage in liturgies of the East and the West, so for ecumenical motives, but also to add another element of participation for the people.[6]

---

1   OR I:94.
2   *Inter oecumenici* DOL 23:48h.
3   Barba, pp. 294 and 648.
4   Barba, p. 481.

5   Barba, pp. 480–481.
6   Barba, pp. 294–295, 481, and 611.

Questions for Discussion and Reflection

1. The embolism expands on the intentions of the Lord's Prayer. How well is this expressed?

_____

_____

_____

2. The priest extends his hands for this prayer. How successful is his gesture?

_____

_____

_____

3. The people respond with an acclamation. How strong is their participation? If the Lord's Prayer is sung, is this acclamation sung? Why or why not?

_____

_____

_____

4. In your community, does the priest remain silent during the people's response?

_____

_____

_____

126.   Then the Priest, with hands extended, says aloud:

Lord Jesus Christ,
who said to your Apostles:
Peace I leave you, my peace I give you;
look not on our sins,
but on the faith of your Church,
and graciously grant her peace and unity
in accordance with your will.

He joins his hands.

Who live and reign for ever and ever.

The people reply:

Amen.

There follows the Rite of Peace, by which the Church entreats peace and unity for herself and for the whole human family, and the faithful express to each other their ecclesial communion and mutual charity before communicating in the Sacrament. . . .

—GIRM, 82

See also GIRM, 181.

Background

The priest addresses Jesus, the giver of peace, and asks for peace on the community. The prayer can be traced to eleventh century. Germany, then to Italy, and finally into the Missal of 1474.[1] The priest originally said it on behalf of himself, "look not on my sins." Throughout this time it immediately preceded the Lamb of God, but the 1970 Missal rearranged the elements of the Communion Rite in order to bring more cohesion to the parts pertaining to prayers for peace. The prayer was retained, but moved forward to a position immediately after the embolism, where it follows up on that prayer's petition for peace and precedes the greeting and sign of peace.[2] The text was put into the first person plural; even though the priest still says the prayer alone, he prays it aloud and on behalf of the community, who respond to it with an Amen.

1   Jungmann 2:330–331.

2   Barba, pp. 298–303.

Questions for Discussion and Reflection

1. The prayer contrasts the sins of those gathered for prayer with the faith of the entire Church. How does your community pray for peace? How do they acknowledge sins that get in the way of peace? Give examples of peace and unity in your community.

_____

_____

_____

2. The priest addresses this prayer to Jesus Christ. Does he use a different gesture for this prayer when he extends his hands? Why or why not?

_____

_____

_____

127.   The Priest, turned towards the people, extending and then joining his hands, adds:

The peace of the Lord be with you always.

The people reply:

And with your spirit.

> Since the celebration of Mass by its nature has a "communitarian" character, both the dialogues between the Priest and the assembled faithful, and the acclamations are of great significance; for they are not simply outward signs of communal celebration but foster and bring about communion between Priest and people.
>
> —GIRM, 34
>
> See also GIRM, 82, 154 and 181.

Background

The priest and the people exchange a brief greeting of peace. A greeting such as this preceded Holy Communion by the eleventh century, where a different formula was in use: "Have the bond of peace and charity, that you may be worthy of the sacred mysteries."[1] People responded together, "May the peace of Christ

1   Jungmann 2:331–332.

and of the Church abound in our hearts."[2] The simpler greeting, "Peace be with you," was in use by the 1474 Missal. The risen Christ spoke this greeting in John's account of the Gospel.[3] The 1570 Missal made this greeting optional, depending on whether or not the peace was exchanged at that Mass. The revised Missal moved the greeting together with the prayer that immediately preceded it ("Lord Jesus Christ") to the position following the embolism, in order to unify the elements of peace prior to the breaking of bread. It also makes the greeting obligatory in all Masses, even if the sign of peace is not exchanged. In this way, the greeting of peace is made at least between the presider and the people.

2 Ibid.
3 See John 20:19, 21, 26.

Questions for Discussion and Reflection

1. This brief greeting brings the prayers for peace into the room in a spoken exchange between the priest and the people. The priest, who was addressing Jesus Christ, now addresses the gathered Church. Does he make a change in voice, eye contact, and gesture? If so, how?

_____

_____

_____

2. How does your community express peace outside the liturgy? How are peace and unity built among those who will gather for worship?

_____

_____

_____

128.   Then, if appropriate, the Deacon, or the Priest, adds:

Let us offer each other the sign of peace.

And all offer one another a sign, in keeping with local customs, that expresses peace, communion, and charity. The Priest gives the sign of peace to a Deacon or minister.

. . . As for the actual sign of peace to be given, the manner is to be established by the Conferences of Bishops in accordance with the culture and customs of the peoples. However, it is appropriate that each person offer the sign of peace, in a sober manner, only to those who are nearest.

—GIRM, 82

See also GIRM, 154 and 181.

Background

A sign of peace may be exchanged by all present. The deacon—or in his absence the priest—extends the invitation. All share peace to those nearby.

The earliest record for the sign of peace comes from Justin, who placed it after the Prayer of the Faithful and just before the bread and wine were brought forward: "When the prayers are concluded we exchange the kiss."[1] This placement was certainly influenced by Matthew 5:23–24, where Jesus admonishes his followers to make peace among themselves before offering their gift at the altar. By the fifth century, however, Innocent recommended a different practice: exchanging the peace after the sacrifice

1 CCC, 1345.

had been made.[2] The people's peace then expressed their consent to what had gone before. After Gregory attached the Lord's Prayer to the conclusion of the canon, the peace naturally slipped into position after it, as an expression of the mutuality implied by that prayer.[3]

Ordo Romanus I instructs the archdeacon to give the peace first to the Bishop, then to the rest in order, and "similarly to the people."[4] But the people's exchange of peace had disappeared from the Mass by the 1474 Missal.

Study Group 10 favored restoring the kiss of peace to the Mass, and did so as an option, although Pope Paul VI considered making it obligatory.[5] At one point the members preferred reinstituting the earlier custom, offering the kiss at the Preparation of the Gifts as an expression of reconciliation, but in the end the group settled on its position following the embolism.[6] The command assigned to the deacon, literally "Offer peace," was taken from the Ambrosian liturgy.[7]

2 *Letter to Decentius of Gubbio*; PL 20:553.
3 Jungmann 2:322–323.
4 OR I:98.

5 Barba, p. 302.
6 Barba, p. 299.
7 Barba, p. 422.

Questions for Discussion and Reflection

1. How is the sign of peace exchanged in your community?

_____

_____

_____

2. With whom does the priest exchange the sign?

_____

_____

_____

3. On what occasions is it offered? Are there some occasions that are considered inappropriate? Why?

_____

_____

_____

4. The sign expresses "peace, communion, and charity." Outside the liturgy, how does your community express those same sentiments?

_____

_____

_____

129. Then he takes the host, breaks it over the paten, and places a small piece in the chalice, saying quietly:

~~May this mingling of the Body and Blood~~
of our Lord Jesus Christ
bring eternal life to us who receive it.

> . . . The Priest breaks the Bread and puts a piece of the host into the chalice to signify the unity of the Body and Blood of the Lord in the work of salvation, namely, of the Body of Jesus Christ, living and glorious. . . .
>
> —GIRM, 83
>
> See also GIRM, 2 and 155.

Background

The priest breaks the host over the paten, places a small piece in the chalice, and offers a prayer that this mingling will bring eternal life to those who receive it.

The practice of reserving part of the consecrated bread from the general Communion appears in the letter of Innocent to Decentius, but even before that, Irenaeus (+202) spoke of sending the Eucharist to other churches.[1] Innocent, as Bishop of Rome, sent some of the consecrated bread from his celebration of the Eucharist to the titular churches around the city. Delivered by acolytes, the particles were given to the priests who presided for other Masses that day. Before Communion, they would drop the particle into the cup, thus establishing eucharistic communion among all the churches of the city with the Bishop of Rome.[2]

As the Church grew, it was impossible to maintain such a practice, but a vestige of it remained. The priest—even the Bishop of Rome—broke off a small piece of the consecrated bread and placed it into his own chalice. The practice probably perdured because of another meaning, that the uniting of the Body and Blood of Christ in the cup served as a sign of the Resurrection.

This interpretation is supported by the text that accompanies the gesture. The text that appeared in *Ordo Romanus I* continued to be used through the Missals of 1474 and 1570: "May the commingling and consecration of the body and blood of our Lord Jesus Christ bring eternal life to us who receive it."[3] By the twentieth century, this text had received some criticism because of its usage of the word "consecration." It seemed to suggest that the consecration of

The priest breaks the host over the paten, places a small piece in the chalice, and offers a prayer that this mingling will bring eternal life to those who receive it.

the elements took place in the commingling.[4] To avoid this misunderstanding, Study Group 10 proposed another text: "May this most holy commingling bring eternal life to us who receive it." This underwent further revisions; the words "body and blood of our Lord Jesus Christ" were restored and "most holy" was removed. The word "consecration" was removed.[5] But the fundamental text was retained because it enjoyed broad usage among Roman and oriental liturgies.[6]

---

1 Eusebius *Historia ecclesiastica* 5:24, 15; SChr 41:71.
2 PL 56:556–557.
3 Translated by Paul Turner.
4 Barba, pp. 305, 611.
5 Barba, pp. 770–771, 841.
6 Barba, p. 422.

Questions for Discussion and Reflection

1. How does the priest break the bread in your community? Is there much bread to be broken?

_____

_____

_____

THE COMMUNIO

2. How clear is the gesture of putting some of the consecrated bread into the cup? Does the priest recite the accompanying text quietly, as instructed?

_____

_____

_____

3. How does your community express its unity with the local Bishop? With the Bishop of Rome?

_____

_____

_____

130.   Meanwhile the following is sung or said:

Lamb of God, you take away the sins of the world,
    have mercy on us.
Lamb of God, you take away the sins of the world,
    have mercy on us.
Lamb of God, you take away the sins of the world,
    grant us peace.

The invocation may even be repeated several times if the fraction is prolonged. Only the final time, however, is **grant us peace** said.

> . . . The gesture of breaking bread done by Christ at the Last Supper, which in apostolic times gave the entire Eucharistic Action its name, signifies that the many faithful are made one body (1 Cor 10:17) by receiving Communion from the one Bread of Life, which is Christ, who for the salvation of the world died and rose again. . . .
>
> —GIRM, 83
>
> See GIRM, 80, 155, 320, 321, and 366.

Background

As the priest breaks the bread, everyone sings or says the Lamb of God. The final invocation returns to the theme of peace that punctuates the ceremonies before Holy Communion.

When the first Christians gathered for the Eucharist, they called their action "the breaking of bread" (Acts of the Apostles 2:42). The significance of the activity gave its name to Eucharistic worship. Tearing bread must have recalled the suffering of Jesus, and sharing it must have recalled the Last Supper. The action served the practical purpose of letting many eat one loaf, but it became imbued with this deeper meaning.

A prayer of thanksgiving from the *Didache* praises God for the "fragment,"[1] which implies a breaking of bread. Gregory the Great kept this action close to Holy Communion by moving the Lord's Prayer closer to the canon.[2]

The fraction is accompanied by the Lamb of God. John the Baptist attributed the title to Jesus.[3] Christ is also called a lamb in 1 Corinthians 5:7, and in Revelation 5:12 and 13:8. According to the *Liber pontificalis*, Pope Sergius introduced the Lamb of God into the Roman Rite, probably having first experienced it in the Antiochene liturgy. "He established that the 'Lamb of God, who take away the sins of the word, have mercy on us' be sung by the clergy and the people at the time of the breaking of the body of the Lord."[4] The repetition of the invocation and the changing of the last line to "grant us peace" were both in practice by the eleventh.[5] In the 1474 and 1570 Missals the fraction preceded the Lamb of God, and the priest struck his breast three times while reciting the text. The gesture was omitted from the

1   *Didache* 9:3; translation PT.
2   PL 77:955–958.
3   John 1:29, 36.
4   LP 1:376; translation PT.
5   Jungmann 2:339.

1970 Missal, and the breaking of bread and singing of the Lamb of God were joined.

The priest is to break the bread into parts so that it can be shared by some of the faithful. He is not to consume all the bread he breaks.[6]

If the breaking takes some time, the invocations may be repeated. Study Group 10 envisioned this option throughout its preparation of the revised rite.[7] The group also proposed eliminating the final petition, "grant us peace," because the peace would already have been exchanged in the Communion Rite, and this was thought a redundancy.[8] However, no change to the text was made after Pope Paul VI explicitly requested that the traditional final petition be retained.[9]

---

6   See GIRM, 321.

7   Barba, pp. 770–771.

8   Barba, p. 422.

9   Barba, p. 675.

Questions for Discussion and Reflection

1. On what occasions does your community sing the Lamb of God? Why?

2. Does the breaking of the bread accompany the music, or does the music sometimes begin during the sign of peace?

3. Does the priest share the pieces of the host he breaks?

4. What kind of bread do you use? Are there other options?

5. Who breaks the bread?

6. On what occasions do you lengthen the Lamb of God?

131. Then the Priest, with hands joined, says quietly:

Lord Jesus Christ, Son of the living God,
who, by the will of the Father
and the work of the Holy Spirit,
through your Death gave life to the world,
free me by this, your most holy Body and Blood,
from all my sins and from every evil;
keep me always faithful to your commandments,
and never let me be parted from you.

Or:

May the receiving of your Body and Blood,
Lord Jesus Christ,
not bring me to judgment and condemnation,
but through your loving mercy
be for me protection in mind and body
and a healing remedy.

The Priest prepares himself by a prayer, said quietly, so that he may fruitfully receive the Body and Blood of Christ. The faithful do the same, praying silently. . . .

—GIRM, 84

See also GIRM, 156.

Background

The priest says a quiet prayer to prepare for receiving Communion. He chooses from two options. The people also pray quietly.

Private prayers of the priest became common in the Middle Ages, and the first of these options, "Lord Jesus Christ, Son of the living God," first appeared in the ninth-century *Sacramentary of Amiens*.[1] The second option first appeared a century later,[2] and surprisingly referred only to receiving the Body of Christ. It alludes to 1 Corinthians 11:29, where Paul warned the faithful not to receive Holy Communion unworthily. Both prayers overtook other options and appeared together in the Missals of 1474 and 1570 immediately following the prayer for peace, "Lord Jesus Christ, you said to your Apostles."

The 1970 Missal introduced some changes. The prayer for peace, as has been seen, was moved earlier in the celebration to the place after the embolism, where it took a harmonious position with other prayers and actions for peace, and where it was now to be recited aloud and rendered in the plural. The other two prayers recited by the priest remained private in preparation for his Holy Communion, but they became alternatives. The texts of these were simplified. The doxology that concluded each of them ("who lives and reigns") was omitted. In the second option, one phrase was struck ("which I, unworthy, presume to receive"), and the words "and Blood" were added. These light retouches made the prayers more fitting within the context of the Communion Rite, focusing the action on more important elements, while helping the priest remain at prayer.

---

1 Jungmann, 2:345.
2 Ibid.

Questions for Discussion and Reflection

1. Does the priest in your community recite his prayer quietly? Which prayer does he choose? Why?

_____

_____

_____

2. Do the people pray quietly with him?

_____

_____

_____

3. How clear is it that spiritual preparation for Communion is happening?

_____

_____

_____

132.   The Priest genuflects, takes the host and, holding it slightly raised above the paten or above the chalice, while facing the people, says aloud:

Behold the Lamb of God,
behold him who takes away the sins of the world.
Blessed are those called to the supper of the Lamb.

And together with the people he adds once:

Lord, I am not worthy
that you should enter under my roof,
but only say the word
and my soul shall be healed.

. . . For this people is the People of God, purchased by Christ's Blood, gathered together by the Lord, nourished by his word, the people called to present to God the prayers of the entire human family, a people that gives thanks in Christ for the mystery of salvation by offering his Sacrifice, a people, finally, that is brought together in unity by Communion in the Body and Blood of Christ. This people, though holy in its origin, nevertheless grows constantly in holiness by conscious, active, and fruitful participation in the mystery of the Eucharist.

—GIRM, 5

See also GIRM, 84 and 157.

Background

Prior to receiving Holy Communion, the people express their unworthiness and pray for healing. The priest invites them to make this statement of faith by showing them the host above the paten or the chalice.

These elements evolved rather late.[1] They began as a way for the people to affirm their faith in the Eucharist prior to receiving it, and to reflect on their unworthiness of so great a sacrament. In the 1474 Missal, the priest said, "Lord, I am not worthy . . ." three times, striking his breast each time. As he held the host for the people to see, and invited them to behold the Lamb of God, he was borrowing elements from the Communion Rite to the sick—which also included a Confiteor. These were adopted into the Communion Rite of the Mass. At the time, the priest received Communion, but the people received infrequently. Their Communion had little connection to the rest of the Mass, and

1   Jungmann 2:371–373.

they received from previously consecrated hosts reserved in the tabernacle, just as the sick did.

The Communion of the people was integrated into the 1970 Missal. The recitation of the

When the people say, "Lord, I am not worthy," the priest joins them to show the communitarian nature of this part of the Mass.

Confiteor was removed because it had become an option for the beginning of Mass. Study Group 10 considered introducing a formula common to oriental Churches, "Holy things for holy people," but this was not accepted.[2] The priest shows the host to the people and announces that those invited to the supper of the Lamb are blessed. When the people say, "Lord, I am not worthy," the priest joins them to show the communitarian nature of this part of the Mass.[3] They all recite the text one time,[4] and striking the breast has been omitted, probably because the gesture seemed superfluous.

The texts are based on several passages from the bible. The priest quotes John the Baptist, who points out the Lamb of God to his disciples.[5] The biblical text says Jesus takes away the "sin" of the world, but the liturgical text has always expressed "sins" in the plural. To this indication is subjoined the statement from Revelation 19:9 that those invited to the supper of the Lamb are blessed. Study Group 10 added this line to the invitation to underscore the eschatological aspect of eucharistic communion.[6]

The response of the entire assembly relies on the story of the healing of the centurion's slave.[7] The biblical words "my child" become the liturgical formula "my soul," probably because the people seek a general spiritual healing more than a specific physical one. Although we are unworthy of Jesus' healing power, he gives himself anyway to those who have faith. Study Group 10 considered changing the biblical word "roof" to the liturgical word "table," but this did not have sufficient support.[8]

---

2   Barba, p. 312.
3   Barba, p. 312.
4   Barba, p. 315.

5   See John 1:29.
6   Barba, p. 313.
7   See Matthew 8:8; Luke 7:6.
8   Barba, pp. 314 and 423.

Questions for Discussion and Reflection

1. The priest genuflects. How is his gesture read by the assembly?

_____

_____

_____

2. The priest shows the consecrated bread to the people, holding it over the paten or over the chalice. Which way happens in your community? Why?

_____

_____

_____

3. How is this gesture different from the ones the priest makes at other parts of the Mass—receiving the gifts, showing the elements during the Institution narrative, and lifting them to conclude the Eucharistic Prayer?

_____

_____

_____

4. Does the priest join the people in the words, "Lord, I am not worthy?" Why would that matter?

_____

_____

_____

5. Outside the liturgy, how else does your community prepare for Holy Communion?

_____

_____

_____

133.   The Priest, facing the altar, says quietly:

May the Body of Christ
keep me safe for eternal life.

And he reverently consumes the Body of Christ.

Then he takes the chalice and says quietly:

May the Blood of Christ
keep me safe for eternal life.

And he reverently consumes the Blood of Christ.

It is most desirable that the faithful, just as the Priest himself is bound to do, receive the Lord's Body from hosts consecrated at the same Mass and that, in the cases where this is foreseen, they partake of the chalice (cf. no. 283), so that even by means of the signs Communion may stand out more clearly as a participation in the sacrifice actually being celebrated.

—GIRM, 85

See also GIRM, 158 and 182.

Background

The priest receives Holy Communion while reciting prayers quietly. He is to receive from the bread and wine consecrated at this Mass.

The texts that accompany the receiving of Holy Communion are fairly late additions to the Mass, coming in the Middle Ages.[1] Various formulas were in use, and none became universal until the 1474 Missal. By that time the two prayers found in the Mass even today appear. The formula can be found, among other places, in John the Deacon's ninth-century life of Gregory.[2] It originated as a prayer the priest said while giving Holy Communion to the sick, but it was imported into the Missal with a change from second person to first ("keep me safe") and for Holy Communion under both kinds.

Starting with the 1474 Missal the priest had two additional devotional prayers to accompany receiving the Body and Blood of Christ, but these were omitted in the 1970 Missal,

The priest receives Holy Communion while reciting prayers quietly.

probably because they seemed a duplication of other material at this time.

Some parts of the Order of Mass still address the rare circumstances when the priest says Mass with his back to the people. The instruction in this case says that he receives Holy Communion "facing the altar." This should be obvious when he stands at a free-standing altar, as envisioned by GIRM, 299.

1   Jungmann 2:355–359.
2   PL 75:103.

Questions for Discussion and Reflection

1. The priest receives Holy Communion "reverently." Is this clear from the actions of the presider?

_____

_____

_____

2. Does the priest recite the texts "quietly"?

_____

_____

_____

3. Does the priest consume an entire large host, or has he broken off parts of it for others to share? Why does this matter?

_____

_____

_____

134.   After this, he takes the paten or ciborium and approaches the communicants. The Priest raises a host slightly and shows it to each of the communicants, saying:

The Body of Christ.

The communicant replies:

Amen.

And receives Holy Communion.

If a Deacon also distributes Holy Communion, he does so in the same manner.

It is most desirable that the faithful. . . partake of the chalice (cf. below, no. 283), so that even by means of the signs Communion will stand out more clearly as a participation in the sacrifice actually being celebrated.

—GIRM, 85

See also GIRM, 80, 86, 87, 182, and 191.

Background

The faithful receive Holy Communion. The deacon and other ministers may assist the priest. In the United States of America, the faithful bow their heads before receiving Holy Communion under each form. The minister says, "The Body of Christ" or "The Blood of Christ," and each person answers, "Amen."

Having deacons assist in the distribution of Holy Communion was practiced in the time of Justin. "When he who presides has given thanks and the people have responded, those whom we call deacons give to those present the 'eucharisted' bread, wine and water and take them to those who are absent."[1] Augustine said that Lawrence the deacon administered the blood of Christ.[2]

The formula, "The Body of Christ" and "The Blood of Christ," and the response to each, "Amen," can be found in the Apostolic Constitutions, where the deacon also administers the chalice.[3] Ambrose wrote,

Therefore you say not casually, "Amen," already confessing in the spirit that you are

1   CCC, 1345.
2   _Sermo_ 304:1, PL 38:1395.
3   AC 8:13,15.

receiving the body of Christ. For when you beg, the priest says to you, "The Body of Christ," and you say, "Amen," that is, "It is true." What the tongue confesses the heart holds.[4]

Augustine knew the same formula. He explained Paul's affirmation that the Corinthians are the body of Christ, members of it.[5]

If therefore you are the body of Christ and members, your mystery has been placed on the Lord's table; you are receiving your mystery. To that which you are, you answer, "Amen," and by responding you agree. For you hear, "The Body of Christ," and you respond, "Amen." Be a member of the body of Christ, so that your "Amen" may be true.[6]

For many centuries, the priest administered Holy Communion to the faithful at Mass using a formula similar to the one in place for Holy Communion to the sick—the same one still in place before his own reception of Holy Communion. In 1964 Pope Paul VI called for this formula to be abbreviated to the one recorded by Ambrose and Augustine.[7] This formula was already in place in the Ambrosian Rite, with which Paul VI was familiar. This change began over the objections of some who believed that a shorter formula could diminish reverence toward the Blessed Sacrament.[8]

The change started by Paul VI continued into the 1970 Missal. Paul had given only the

> The minister says, "The Body of Christ" or "The Blood of Christ," and each person answers, "Amen."

formula for administering the Body of Christ, probably because it was rare to administer the cup to the faithful. The Order of Mass to this day only supplies the complete text for administering Holy Communion under one form to the faithful: "The Body of Christ." The words "The Blood of Christ" are merely implied by the following paragraph.

---

4   *De Sacramentis* 4:25, SChr 25b:116–117; translation PT.
5   See 1 Corinthians 12:27.
6   *Sermo* 272, PL 38:1247; translation PT.

7   *Inter oecumenici*, 48i; DOL 23.
8   Barba, p. 46.

Questions for Discussion and Reflection

1. What is the procedure for the distribution of Holy Communion with your community? How would you evaluate it for reverence, efficiency, and meaning?

_____

_____

_____

2. Who distributes Holy Communion in your community? How have they been prepared? How is their ministry regarded by other members of the community?

_____

_____

_____

3. How familiar are people with the proper way to receive Holy Communion? Do they hold their hands correctly? If receiving Holy Communion on the tongue, do they help the minister place the consecrated bread there in a simple manner? Do they bow their heads before receiving? Do they say "Amen" with a strong voice?

_____

_____

_____

135. If any are present who are to receive Holy Communion under both kinds, the rite described in the proper place is to be followed.

Holy Communion has a fuller form as a sign when it takes place under both kinds. For in this form the sign of the Eucharistic banquet is more clearly evident and clearer expression is given to the divine will by which the new and eternal Covenant is ratified in the Blood of the Lord, as also the connection between the Eucharistic banquet and the eschatological banquet in the Kingdom of the Father.

—GIRM, 281

See also GIRM, 14, 85, 160, 161, 182, 191, and 282–287.

Background

Holy Communion may be distributed under both kinds to the faithful in order to emphasize the full meaning of the eucharistic banquet.

At the Last Supper, of course, Jesus asked all of those present to drink from the cup. The Church therefore never eliminated the possibility of administering Holy Communion under both forms to the faithful. However, during the Middle Ages, the cup was reserved to the clergy, largely out of fear of spillage stemming from a heightened sense of the real presence of Christ in the Eucharist. The Second Vatican Council permitted the broader reception of Holy Communion from the cup, and the practice has spread with enthusiasm and appreciation from the faithful in many parts of the world.

Questions for Discussion and Reflection

1. On what occasion does your community have Holy Communion under both kinds? Who administers the cup?

_____

_____

_____

2. Do many of the faithful take advantage of Holy Communion under both kinds? Why or why not?

_____

_____

_____

136. While the Priest is receiving the Body of Christ, the Communion Chant begins.

While the Priest is receiving the Sacrament, the Communion Chant is begun, its purpose being to express the spiritual union of the communicants by means of the unity of their voices, to show gladness of heart, and to bring out more clearly the "communitarian" character of the procession to receive the Eucharist. . . .

—GIRM, 86

See also GIRM, 87 and 159.

Background

The people sing a song for the Communion procession. It begins with the communion of the priest in order to unite his communion with that of the rest of the assembly. A text is recommended each day in the Missal, but others may be chosen.

Evidence for singing Psalms during Holy Communion is quite ancient. The *Apostolic Constitutions* say, "the thirty-third Psalm is said while all the rest receive communion."[1] In one of his mystagogical catecheses, Cyril of Jerusalem (+386) wrote,

> After that you hear the song that invites you with a divine melody to communion of the holy mysteries: "Taste and see that the Lord is good." Do not trust the judgment of your corporal palate, but of undoubtable faith. For in tasting, this is not bread and wine that you taste, but the body and blood of Christ that they signify.[2]

The custom continued, as evidenced by *Ordo Romanus I*:

> As soon as the bishop begins to receive communion in the sanctuary, the choir immediately starts the Communion Antiphon (at times with the subdeacons), and they sing the psalm until, all the people having received Communion, the bishop nods to indicate that they should sing the Glory to the Father, and then, having repeated the verse, they stop.[3]

The 1970 Missal restored the practice of starting the Communion music with the presider's reception of Holy Communion. It was designed to unify the communion of the priest and the people,[4] but it also restored an ancient Roman practice.

---

1 AC 8:13, 16; translation PT.

2 SChr 126:168–171; translation PT.
3 OR I:117; translation PT.
4 Barba, p. 320.

Questions for Discussion and Reflection

1. When does the Communion music begin in your community?

_____

_____

_____

2. How do you choose what to sing? Who makes the choice? Are the antiphons in the Missal consulted?

_____

_____

_____

3. Is there always music during Holy Communion? On what occasions do you sing or not sing? Why?

_____

_____

_____

137.　When the distribution of Communion is over, the Priest or a Deacon or an acolyte purifies the paten over the chalice and also the chalice itself.

While he carries out the purification, the Priest says quietly:

What has passed our lips as food, O Lord,
may we possess in purity of heart,
that what has been given to us in time
may be our healing for eternity.

When the distribution of Communion is over, the Deacon returns to the altar with the Priest, collects the fragments, should any remain, and then carries the chalice and other sacred vessels to the credence table, where he purifies them and arranges them as usual, while the Priest returns to the chair. Nevertheless, it is also permitted to leave vessels needing to be purified on a corporal, suitably covered, on the credence table, and to purify them immediately after Mass, following the Dismissal of the people.

—GIRM, 183

See also GIRM, 163, 171, 192, 278-280, 284, and 334.

Background

Following Holy Communion, the particles and droplets of the consecrated bread and wine are collected and consumed by a priest, deacon, or instituted acolyte.

The earliest record of the prayer for the priest to say is a generic post-Communion prayer in the *Veronese Sacramentary*, and the words have virtually remained unchanged since the sixth century. The text appears in the 1474 Missal. In the 1570 Missal, it appears with instructions for purifying the vessels. The priest extended the chalice toward a minister who poured a little wine into it, while the priest said another prayer. The priest washed and dried his fingers and drank the liquid from the chalice. He then dried his mouth and the chalice.

Study Group 10 simplified these actions, retaining the reverence of the purification and clarifying its purpose.[1] Wine is no longer used. The revised ceremony kept the first prayer, which is still said quietly by the priest when he purifies the vessels.

1　Barba, p. 316.

Questions for Discussion and Reflection

1. How is the purification of vessels conducted in your community?

_____

_____

_____

2. Does it take place after Holy Communion or after Mass? Why? Who performs the purification?

_____

_____

3. Does the purification take place on the altar or at the side table? Why?

_____

_____

_____

138.   Then the Priest may return to the chair. If appropriate, a sacred silence may be observed for a while, or a psalm or other canticle of praise or a hymn may be sung.

> When the distribution of Communion is over, if appropriate, the Priest and faithful pray quietly for some time. If desired, a Psalm or other canticle of praise or a hymn may also be sung by the whole congregation.
>
> —GIRM, 88
>
> See also GIRM, 43 and 164.

Background

After Holy Communion the priest may return to his chair—or go to the altar. Silence may be observed. All may sing praise to God. Now that individuals have received Holy Communion, all observe silence or song together as the body of Christ.

In general, periods of silence for the entire assembly are fresh additions to the Mass.[1] There is no clear historical precedent for them. However, there is a record of a post-Communion song in the time of Sergius of Constantinople (+638):

> Let this antiphon be sung: Let our mouth be filled with praise, Lord, that we may celebrate your glory, for you have graciously given us your holy mysteries. Keep

us in holiness, meditating all day on your justice. Alleluia.[2]

Study Group 10 proposed having the priest return to his chair after Holy Communion. Formerly, he returned to the altar. The new location was chosen that "the whole arrangement of the final rites of the mass could be done in greater order."[3]

More seriously, the group had to decide how the Mass would end. With the removal of the Last Gospel and the final prayers of the Mass, members received some criticism that Mass was ending rather abruptly. The insertion of a period of time after Communion for silent thanksgiving or a hymn of praise addressed these issues.[4]

_____

1   Cabié, *The Church at Prayer*, 2:219.

2   *Chronicon Paschale*, PG 92:1001–1002; translation PT.

3   Barba, p. 316.

4   Barba, pp. 317 and 482.

Questions for Discussion and Reflection

1. How does your community spend the time after Holy Communion? On what occasions do you sing?

_____

_____

_____

2. If you observe silence, how long does it last? Who gives the cue for it to end?

_____

_____

_____

3. Some of the faithful probably leave Mass early. Is there a problem with the quality of the time after Holy Communion?

_____

_____

_____

---

139.   Then, standing at the altar or at the chair and facing the people, with hands joined, the Priest says:

Let us pray.

All pray in silence with the Priest for a while, unless silence has just been observed. Then the Priest, with hands extended, says the Prayer after Communion, at the end of which the people acclaim:

Amen.

> To bring to completion the prayer of the People of God, and also to conclude the whole Communion Rite, the Priest pronounces the Prayer after Communion, in which he prays for the fruits of t,he mystery just celebrated. . . .
>
> —GIRM, 89
>
> See also GIRM, 30, 165, and 184.

Background

The Prayer after Communion concludes the Communion Rite, summing up its purpose in a single prayer to God. The priest leads the prayer, and the people respond, "Amen."

Early evidence for such a prayer can be found in the *Apostolic Constitutions*, where the deacon invites the assembly to give thanks to Christ, "who has made us worthy to be sharers of his holy mysteries."[1] Examples abound in the *Veronese* and *Gelasian Sacramentaries*, where the concise prayer for this part of the Roman tradition took shape. Together with the Collect and the prayer over the offerings, the Prayer after Communion joined the set of presidential prayers.

In the centuries before the Second Vatican Council, it was customary to use more than one Prayer after Communion; for example, one for the saint's day and one for the season. But the revised Missal limits this to just one prayer,[2] which gives clearer focus and direction to the Communion Rite.

It had also been the custom for the priest to greet the people again before this prayer. Study Group 10 considered retaining "The Lord be with you" here, but abandoned it in favor of starting directly with the instruction "Let us pray."[3]

1   AC 8:14; translation PT.

2   GIRM, 89; Barba, p. 320.
3   Barba, pp. 320–321.

Now that silence had been introduced as an option before the Prayer after Communion, it was not clear if silence should follow the admonition, "Let us pray." The revised Missal says that if silence precedes the invitation to prayer, it need not follow.[4]

It had been the custom for the priest to lead this prayer from the altar, but the 1970 Missal gave him the option of moving to the chair, and

listed it as the first, or preferred, alternative. The third edition of *The Roman Missal*, however, reversed the sequence of these options, allowing the priest to stand either at the altar or the chair. It is not clear if the reversal of choices represents the historical tradition or a new preference.

The Prayer after Communion concludes the Communion Rite, summing up its purpose in a single prayer to God.

4 Barba, p. 321.

Questions for Discussion and Reflection

1. When does silence happen in your community—before or after the words, "Let us pray"?

_____

_____

_____

2. On what occasions does the priest sing the Prayer after Communion?

_____

_____

_____

3. Where does the priest stand for this prayer? Why?

_____

_____

_____

THE CONCLUDING RITES

ANNOUNCEMENTS

140. If they are necessary, any brief announcements to the people follow here.

> Once the prayer after Communion has been said, the Deacon makes brief announcements to the people, if indeed any need to be made, unless the Priest prefers to do this himself.
>
> —GIRM, 184
>
> See also GIRM, 90 and 166.

Background

Once the Communion Rite concludes, and just preceding the final blessing and dismissal, announcements for the sake of the community may be made. These help the people know how to live out the Gospel in the coming week.

Logically, a community gathering regularly always needs announcements. People need to know where and when to meet the next time, and to exchange information pertinent to their upcoming activities. In *Ordo Romanus I*, just before giving Holy Communion to the faithful, the archdeacon announced the day for the next celebration, the name of the church, and whether it was inside or outside the city walls. People answered "Thanks be to God" to this announce-ment.[1] Similarly, before the reception of Holy Communion, the *Gelasian Sacramentary* calls for announcements about days of fast, prebaptismal rites, prayers for the sick, and the feast days of the saints.[2] It makes one wonder if announcements preceded Holy Communion because people left the celebration early.

In modern times a custom developed for making the announcements part of the homily at the parish Mass. By assigning the announcements a certain time, the Order of Mass expresses its preference that they not interrupt the flow of the Communion Rite, but stand at the head of the dismissal, suggesting purposes for sending the assembly into the world. Repeatedly the GIRM asks that they be brief, and made only if necessary.

---

1   OR I:108.
2   Gelasian 1260.

Questions for Discussion and Reflection

1. When are the announcements made in your parish community?

_____

_____

_____

2. Who makes them? Who writes them?

_____

_____

_____

3. What are your local guidelines for what may and may not be announced?

_____

_____

4. How do you distinguish the purpose of the announcements from the purpose of the bulletin or the Web site?

_____

_____

_____

FINAL BLESSING

141.   Then the dismissal takes place. The Priest, facing the people and extending his hands, says:

The Lord be with you.

The people reply:

And with your spirit.

The Priest blesses the people, saying:

May almighty God bless you,
the Father, and the Son, ✛ and the Holy Spirit.

The people reply:

Amen.

Then the Priest, extending his hands, greets the people, saying, *The Lord be with you*. They reply *And with your spirit*. The Priest, joining his hands again and then immediately placing his left hand on his breast, raises his right hand and adds, *May Almighty God bless you* and, as he makes the Sign of the Cross over the people, he continues, *the Father, and the Son, and the Holy Spirit*. All reply, *Amen*. . . .

—GIRM, 167

See also GIRM, 31, 90, 92 and 185.

Background

Before dismissing the people, the priest offers them his blessing. In Masses with a deacon, these are the priest's final words to the rest of the assembly.

The blessing probably started as a devotional practice when the Bishop blessed individuals after the service. In the fourth century, Egeria witnessed a procession of people coming to the Bishop in Jerusalem for an individual blessing, but not during the Eucharist.[1] The Bishop also blessed the faithful on Sundays at what appears to be the close of a Eucharist, and then individuals came to him, probably to kiss his hand.[2] In one sermon, Caesarius of Arles (+542) admonished those who did not stay for the entire Mass, and mentioned the custom of the blessing: "Therefore, those who want to celebrate the mass completely with profit for their souls should keep themselves in the church with a humbled body and a contrite heart until the Lord's Prayer is said and the blessing for the people is given."[3] In *Ordo Romanus I* the Pope gives a blessing to other Bishops in the sacristy immediately after the Eucharist. They ask him for a blessing, and he says, "May the Lord bless us." They answer, "Amen."[4] The text in use today can be found in the acts from the Synod of Albi in 1230.[5] The 1474 Missal called for a blessing before the final prayer, and the 1570 Missal placed it after the dismissal. Again it seems to have grown from the practice of blessing individuals after the Mass.

The 1970 Missal rearranged these parts more logically, moving the dismissal formula to the end of the Mass, and letting the blessing follow the Prayer after Communion. In this way, the priest gives his blessing over the people, a kind of farewell gesture, just before the deacon dismisses the assembly.

---

1   *Diary of Egeria* 24:2. Wilkinson, p. 143.
2   *Diary of Egeria* 25:2. Wilkinson, p. 145.
3   *Sermo_73*:2. CCL 103:307; translation PT.
4   OR I:126; translation PT.
5   Jungmann 2:444.

Questions for Discussion and Reflection

1. The priest makes the Sign of the Cross over the people. How deliberate is his gesture? Do his words have a sense of finality about them?

_____

_____

_____

2. In most congregations, the people sign themselves with the cross. The rubrics never mention this, but the custom is widespread. What is your custom and why?

_____

_____

_____

SOLEMN BLESSING

142.   On certain days or occasions, this formula of blessing is preceded, in accordance with the rubrics, by another more solemn formula of blessing or by a prayer over the people . . . .

> To the Concluding Rites belong the following: . . the Priest's Greeting and Blessing, which on certain days and occasions is expanded and expressed by the Prayer over the People or another more solemn formula; . . .
>
> —GIRM, 90b
>
> See GIRM, 167 and 185.

Background

On certain days the blessing may be amplified in one of two ways. A Solemn Blessing is a three-fold prayer in the third person ("May almighty God . . .") to which the people answer "Amen" after each part. The Prayer over the People is a single prayer addressed to God, concluding with a formula, to which the people answer, "Amen." A deacon asks the faithful to bow their heads immediately after the greeting of the priest.

In the fourth-century _Apostolic Constitutions_ the deacon asks the people to bow their heads for this blessing.[1]

The _Gregorian Sacramentary_ gives multiple examples of a Prayer over the People for the season of Lent. The _Veronese_ and _Gelasian Sacramentaries_ have examples at other times of the year. The _Gregorian Sacramentary_ also has a selection of blessings divided into parts, separated by an Amen from the people.[2] These are forerunners of the threefold Solemn Blessing the 1970 Missal put into use.

Study Group 10 proposed having 3 forms of blessing for the end of Mass: the ordinary form currently in force; an extraordinary form based on the _Gregorian Sacramentary_, in turn inspired by the threefold blessing of Aaron;[3] and the Prayer over the People.[4] This solution was adopted.

---

1   AC 15:6.

2   _Le Sacramentaire Grégorien_, Ed. Jean Deshusses (Freiburg: Éditions Universitaires Fribourg Suisse, 1979) I:1738–1789.

3   See Numbers 6:24–25.

4   Barba, p. 364.

Questions for Discussion and Reflection

1. On what occasions does your community use the various forms of the final blessing?

_____

_____

_____

2. Does a deacon invite people to bow their heads?

_____

_____

_____

3. How does your community determine which blessing it will hear?

_____

_____

_____

4. Is the blessing ever sung? Does that help the people make their response?

_____

_____

_____

FINAL BLESSING AT A PONTIFICAL MASS

143. In a Pontifical Mass, the celebrant receives the miter and, extending his hands, says:

The Lord be with you.

All reply:

And with your spirit.

The celebrant says:

Blessed be the name of the Lord.

All reply:

Now and for ever.

. . . A Bishop blesses the people with the appropriate formula, making the Sign of the Cross three times over the people.

—GIRM, 167

See also GIRM, 92.

The celebrant says:

Our help is in the name of the Lord.

All reply:

Who made heaven and earth.

Then the celebrant receives the pastoral staff, if he uses it, and says:

May almighty God bless you,

making the Sign of the Cross over the people three times, he adds:

the Father, ✠ and the Son, ✠ and the Holy ✠ Spirit.

All:

Amen.

Background

When a Bishop gives the final blessing, there are slight changes in its text and gestures. He involves the people in an additional dialogue. He makes the Sign of the Cross three times as he mentions the Persons of the Trinity.

Durandus (+1296) restricted to Bishops the use of the versicle, "Blessed be the name of the Lord."[1] The text comes from Psalm 113:2. The second versicle, "Our help is in the name of the

Lord," can be found in the *Salzburg Missal* from around the same era.[2] The text comes from Psalm 124:8. The use of multiple Signs of the Cross can be found in a Sacramentary of the eleventh century from Bologna.[3]

Today, many people are unfamiliar with the brief dialogue that precedes the Bishop's blessing, simply because they rarely participate at Mass with him. But his texts and gestures remain in force after many centuries of usage.

---

1   *Rationale* 4:59, 7; see Jungmann 2:444; translation PT.

2   Jungmann 2:444.

3   Jungmann 2:444–445.

Questions for Discussion and Reflection

1. How well does your assembly know the responses to the dialogue preceding the blessing by a Bishop? On what occasion might instruction be useful?

_____

_____

_____

2. When the Bishop administers his blessing, how would you describe its effect?

_____

_____

_____

3. Outside the liturgy, in what ways are the people of your community connected to the Bishop? When are they in his presence? How do they share his mission?

_____

_____

_____

DISMISSAL

144. Then the Deacon, or the Priest himself, with hands joined and facing the people, says:

Go forth, the Mass is ended.

Or:

Go and announce the Gospel of the Lord.

Or:

Go in peace, glorifying the Lord by your life.

Or:

Go in peace.

The people reply:

Thanks be to God.

> . . . After the Priest's blessing, the Deacon, with hands joined and facing the people, dismisses the people, saying the *Ite, missa est* (*Go forth, the Mass is ended*).
>
> —GIRM, 185
>
> See also GIRM, 90 and 168.

Background

The final dialogue of the Mass is begun by the deacon, who sends the people forth from the Eucharist into the world. During the Mass the deacon directs the people to perform certain actions; now he invites them to the kind of service he himself will offer the Church in the week to come.

In the fourth-century *Apostolic Constitutions*, the deacon closes the liturgy with the words, "Go in peace."[1] No response for the people is recorded there. The deacon's words may have come from Mark 5:34, where Jesus uses them to end a conversation with the healed woman who touched his garment in the midst of a crowd. A different formula, "Go, [the assembly] is dismissed," said by the archdeacon, with

the people's response, "Thanks be to God," appears in *Ordo Romanus I*.[2] This formula has endured to this day, although it was missing from the 1474 Missal.

The words *Ite, missa est* could have originated in a secular context, as a formula to announce the conclusion of a meeting.[3] But gradually the word "missa" was adopted as the name of the entire preceding celebration, rendered in English as "Mass." The Latin word is also the root for "Missal," the title of the book containing the texts and rubrics for the celebration of the Eucharist.

As Study Group 10 was preparing the Order of Mass, the members desired to make the dismissal a true dismissal formula, moving it from

_____

1   AC 8:15, 10; translation PT.

2   OR I:124; translation PT.

3   Cabié, *The Church at Prayer*, 2:123.

its position before the final blessing to become the last dialogue of the Mass. Other elements that had been added to the end of the Mass over the years were to be eliminated, thus restoring the dismissal's proper function. The group realized that vernacular languages would need to express the Latin words *Ite, missa est* with some freedom, in order to grasp its meaning and to accent its valedictory function.[4]

After the third edition of *The Roman Missal* was published in Latin in 2002, the Vatican expanded the formulas for the dismissal, apparently inspired by Pope Benedict's closing address to the 2005 Synod of Bishops in Rome.[5] In *The Sacramentary* in English, several formulas had existed for use in the United States, and many deacons interpreted these as carrying the rubric, "in these or similar words." The rubric has still not returned, but a selection of dismissal formulas was approved for insertion in the 2008 emended publication of the Latin third edition of *The Roman Missal*.

---

4 Barba, pp. 364 and 567.

5 See http://www.vatican.va/holy_father/benedict_xvi/ speeches/2005/october/documents/hf_ben_xvi_ spe_20051022_pranzo-sinodo_en.html.

Questions for Discussion and Reflection

1. How is the assembly dismissed from the liturgy? What words are chosen?

_____

_____

_____

2. Who issues the dismissal in your community? Does the personal service of the priest or deacon lend additional meaning to the charge to go forth?

_____

_____

_____

3. On what occasions is this formula sung?

_____

_____

_____

4. Double Alleluias conclude both elements of the dismissal formula throughout the Octave of Easter and on the solemnity of Pentecost. Are these observed in your community? Are they sung?

_____

_____

_____

VENERATION OF THE ALTAR, PROCESSION, AND CLOSING HYMN

145. Then the Priest venerates the altar as usual with a kiss, as at the beginning. After making a profound bow with the ministers, he withdraws.

> . . . As to the other sacred actions and all the activities of the Christian life, these are bound up with it, flow from it, and are ordered to it.
>
> —GIRM, 16
>
> See also GIRM, 90, 169, 186, and 274.

Background

The priest and deacon kiss the altar, bow to the sanctuary—or genuflect if the tabernacle is there—and withdraw. The rubrics do not indicate it, but the people also make a reverence to the altar or the tabernacle, and then leave to serve the Church in the world.

The ninth-century *Sacramentary of Amiens* in France records the practice of the priest kissing the altar,[1] but there is not much evidence earlier than this. It probably originated as a farewell kiss to balance the one at the beginning of Mass. Some have argued that in the kiss, the priest received the blessing of Christ, whom the altar represents, and then extended it to the community with his greeting, but not all agree.[2] In the 1570 Missal the kissing of the altar preceded the final blessing. However, it has been placed after the dismissal as the final act of the ministers before leaving the sanctuary. Study Group 10 proposed a rubric that did not survive the final editing of the Order of Mass: "Then the priest with the ministers, the rightful reverence to the altar having been made, withdraw, and all return to their good works, together praising God."[3]

It has become customary to sing a closing hymn or song. However, the GIRM and the Order of Mass never mention it.[4] There is scant evidence for such a practice in history, natural though it feels. Perhaps the shortening of the Concluding Rites of the Mass created a void that worshippers felt should be filled by singing another hymn. As with the kiss of the altar, it creates a balance with the actions at the beginning of the Mass.

---

1 Jungmann 2:437.
2 Ibid.

3 Barba, p. 510.
4 The recent music document from the USCCB, *Sing to the Lord: Music in Divine Worship* (199), and the USCCB document, *Introduction to the Order of Mass* (165), recognizes that it has become a custom to sing a closing hymn in the United States of America.

Questions for Discussion and Reflection

1. What reverence do the ministers and the people show upon leaving the church? Do they genuflect to the tabernacle or bow to the altar? Why?

_____

_____

_____

2. Is it customary for your community to sing a closing hymn or song? Why? Does instrumental music ever replace the closing hymn?

_____

_____

_____

RITES FOLLOWING MASS

146. If any liturgical action follows immediately, the rites of dismissal are omitted.

If, however, another liturgical action follows the Mass, the Concluding Rites, that is, the Greeting, the Blessing, and the Dismissal, are omitted.

—GIRM, 170

Background

In the instances when Mass is followed by another rite, the elements of the dismissal are omitted, or more accurately deferred until the entire celebration is complete. This happens commonly at a funeral Mass. Following the Prayer after Communion, the liturgy continues with the final commendation, not with the greeting, blessing, and dismissal.

Questions for Discussion and Reflection

1. On what occasions does another liturgical rite follow the Mass in your community?

_____

_____

_____

2. How is the transition made?

_____

_____

_____

Afterword

Prayer is simple. It is experiencing the love of God. It is the stopping of other things so that the heart can know its maker.

The celebration of the Mass is the Church's most important prayer. It has attracted an elaborate panoply of words and gestures, songs, and silences, to express and experience what we hold most dear—the real presence of Jesus Christ.

Those who work through this book will find themselves either more distracted or more involved at Mass. That is the risk of analyzing prayer.

If you place yourself at prayer whenever you are at Mass, all else will disappear. It will be you, the community of the faithful, and Christ, who invites you to be his Body at the supper of the Lamb.

Bibliography

Barba, Maurizio. *La riforma conciliare dell' "Ordo Missae": Il percorso storico-redazionale dei riti d'ingresso, di offertorio e di comunione*. Rome, Italy: Edizioni Liturgiche CLV, 2008.

Botte, Bernard, and Mohrmann, Christine. *L'Ordinaire de la messe*. Études Liturgiques. Paris, France: Les editions du Cerf, 1953.

Bradshaw, Paul; Johnson, Maxwell E.; and Phillips, L. Edward. *The Apostolic Tradition: A Commentary*. Ed. Harold W. Attridge. Minneapolis, Minnesota: Augsburg Fortress, 2002.

Cabié, Robert. *History of the Mass*. Trans. Lawrence J. Johnson. Portland, Oregon: Pastoral Press, 1992.

Catechism of the Catholic Church for the United States of America © 1994 United States Catholic Conference, Inc.—Libreria Editrice Vaticana. English translation of the *Catechism of the Catholic Church Modifications from the Editio Typica* © 1997, United States Catholic Conference, Inc.—Libreria Editrice Vaticana.

The Church at Prayer: An Introduction to the Liturgy. Ed. Aimé Georges Martimort. Collegeville, Minnesota: Liturgical Press, 1992.

Deiss, Lucien. *The Mass*. Collegeville, Minnesota: Liturgical Press, 1992.

Didache. Anton Hänggi-Irmgard Pahl, *Prex eucharistica Frieburg*. Éditions Universitaires Fribourg Suisse, 1968, pp. 66–69.

Didascalia et Constitutiones Apostolorum. Ed. Franciscus Xaverius Funk. Turin, Italy: Bottega d'Erasmo, 1979.

Egeria's Travels. Trans. John Wilkinson; 3rd edition. Warminster, England: Aris & Phillips, Ltd, 1999.

Foley, Edward. *From Age to Age: How Christians Have Celebrated the Eucharist, Revised and Expanded Edition*. Collegeville, Minnesota: Liturgical Press, 2008.

Fortescue, Adrian. *The Mass: A Study of the Roman Liturgy*. London, England: Longmans, Green and Co., 1950.

Jeffrey, Peter. "The Meanings and Functions of *Kyrie eleison*." *The Place of Christ in Liturgical Prayer: Trinity, Christology, and Liturgical Theology*. Ed. Bryan D. Spinks. Collegeville, Minnesota: Liturgical Press, 2008, pp. 127–194.

Johnson, Lawrence J. *The Mystery of Faith: A Study of the Structural Elements of the Order of Mass, Revised Edition 2004*. Washington, DC: Federation of Diocesan Liturgical Commissions, 2004.

Jungmann, Joseph A. *The Mass of the Roman Rite: Its Origins and Development (Missarum Sollemnia)*. Trans. Francis A. Brunner. Westminster, Maryland: Christian Classics, Inc., 1992.

Klauser, Theodor. *A Short History of the Western Liturgy: An Account and Some Reflections, Second Edition*. Oxford, England: Oxford University Press, 1979.

Liber pontificalis, Le. Ed. L. Duchesne. Paris, France: E. de Boccard, 1955.

Mazza, Enrico; translated by Matthew J. O'Connell. *The Eucharistic Prayers of the Roman Rite.* New York, New York: Pueblo Publishing Co., 1986.

Neunheuser, Burkhard. *Storia della liturgia attraverso le epoche culturali.* Rome, Italy: CLV Edizioni Liturgiche, 1983.

Nocent, Adrien. *La Messe avant et après Saint Pie V.* Paris, France: Editions Beauchesne, 1977.

Les Ordines Romani du haut moyen age. Ed. Michel Andrieu. Louvain, Belgium: Spicilegium Sacrum Lovaniense, 1971.

Oury, Guy. *La Messe de S. Pei V à Paul VI.* Solesmes, 1975.

Parenti, Stefano. "Lo Studio e la storia della messa Romana nella prospettiva della liturgia comparata: Alcuni esempi." *Ecclesia Orans* 25 (2008):193–226.

Raffa, Vincenzo. *Liturgia eucaristica: Mistagogia della Messa: dalla storia e dalla teologia alla pastorale pratica.* Rome, Italy: Edizioni Liturgiche CLV, 2003.

Turner, Paul. *Let Us Pray: A Guide to the Rubrics of Sunday Mass.* A Pueblo Book. Collegeville, Minnesota: Liturgical Press, 2006.

Wapelhorst, Innocent. *Compendium sacrae liturgiae juxta Ritum Romanum.* New York, New York: Benziger Brothers, 1925.

Ward, Anthony. "Euchology for the Mass 'In Cena Domini' of the 2000 *Missale Romanum*." *Notitiae* 507–508 (December 2008, 11–12):611–634.